The Year 2030 in Prophecy

A proof of the Bible

This book analyzes Biblical scriptures and prophetic timelines in the context of contemporary world affairs. It aims to demonstrate that Jesus Christ is the sole Messiah and that the Bible remains enduringly relevant.

By Pieter C Voges

2030 in Prophecy

Disclaimer

© 2023, Author P. Voges

This eBook is designed to provide information and motivation to our readers. It may contain links to other websites or content belonging to or originating from third parties or links to websites and features. Such external links are not investigated, monitored, or checked for accuracy, adequacy, validity, reliability, availability, or completeness.

All information in these eBooks is provided in good faith; however, we make no representation or warranty of any kind, express or implied, regarding the accuracy, adequacy, validity, reliability, availability, or completeness of any information.

The photos are provided to assist in comprehension but are not from actual events. They are from royalty-free stock photos.

All rights reserved. No part of this publication may be reproduced or used in any form or by any means—electronic or mechanical, including photocopying, recording, or information storage and retrieval systems.

Grammarly gen AI was used to audit and enhance the writing for American English, thereby improving the writing style for that market.

Contents

Introduction

The Gospel accounts record Jesus proclaiming that He would fulfill the sign of Jonah. Just as Jonah spent three days and nights in the belly of the great fish, Jesus would also be in the heart of the earth before His resurrection. While many interpret the prophecy as ending here, the text offers further implications.

The book of Jonah contains End Times prophecies! It indicates what will happen in the Last Days and when! Consider the sign as Jesus Christ explained:

> "Then certain of the scribes and of the Pharisees answered, saying, Master, we want to see a sign from you.
> But He answered and said to them, An evil and adulterous generation seeks after a sign. And there shall be no sign given to it except the sign of the Prophet Jonah.
> For as Jonah was three days and three nights in the belly of the huge fish, so the Son of Man shall be three days and three nights in the heart of the earth."
> (Matthew 12:38-40, MKJV)

Jesus fulfilled that sign. He was miraculously resurrected after three days and three nights, or 72 hours, to be exact. Moreover, we may think that that is all there is to it. There is a lot more than meets the eye!

There are many more similarities between this event in the life of the Prophet Jonah and Jesus's ministry. The events of Jonah's ministry are a prophecy for us as well. The ultimate Messianic fulfillment extends to 2030. In world events, we are nearing that point.

God wants us to be informed beforehand so that when it happens, we know it was written for us thousands of years ago. It establishes the authority of Jesus Christ in world events.

Chapter 1

Prophetic Principles

Exact physical fulfilment

To understand and anticipate the place in history the year 2030 will hold, we must first consider the prophetic principles of the Bible. At times, the Bible is direct. It states the years exactly. It means what it says. Notice the following example below.

Keep in mind that because of Israel's disrespect and disobedience, God declared at that time that Israel would lose their inheritance and would go into captivity for 70 years. Babylon will overrun and ruin the land of Israel, and in particular Jerusalem. As a result, the land of Israel will be undeveloped for 70 years.

> "This entire land will be a desolation and a waste, and these nations will serve the king of Babylon for seventy years.
>
> Then when the seventy years have passed, I'll judge the king of Babylon and that nation, declares the LORD, I'll judge the land of the Chaldeans for their iniquity and I'll make it a desolation forever."
>
> (Jeremiah 25:11-12, ISV)

This exactly happened as prophesied. Israel was destroyed, the people were taken captive, and the land laid waste for 70 years. Afterward, Babylon were destroyed and never rebuilt to its former glory. However, Jerusalem was prophesied to be rebuilt.

The prophet Daniel was in the king's court in Babylon when the words of the Lord came to him about the restoration of Jerusalem.

> "in the first year of his reign, I, Daniel, understood the number of the years by books, which came of the Word of Jehovah to Jeremiah the prophet, that he would accomplish seventy years in the desolations of Jerusalem."

(Daniel 9:2, MKJV)

The restoration of Jerusalem began after 70 years, as promised by God. Even today, Jerusalem is still a significant city. However, Babylon would fall as promised. Even its religious system would be impeded in the ruins of Babylon at that time. But the Temple in Jerusalem would be rebuilt and continue to function as intended in the Old Testament for over a thousand more years till Messiah came.

Isaiah also prophesied about Babylon's demise. Any attempt at rebuilding the city of Babylon would not last.

> "Look! Here come riders, each man with a pair of horses!" They're shouting out the answer: "Babylon has fallen, has fallen, and they have shattered all the images of her gods on the ground!"

(Isaiah 21:9, MKJV)

This happened in dramatic fashion, and the event is described in the history books forever.

Spiritual fulfilment

At times, there may be spiritual a fulfillment. In the case of Babylon, its religious concepts and ways, deception and falseness, were still evident among many nations. In the Last Days, when the power of the English-speaking nations will decline, it will come to the fore again, only to be destroyed in the end.

"Then another angel, a second one, followed him, saying, "Fallen! Babylon the Great has fallen! She has made all nations drink the wine, the wrath earned for her sexual sins.""

(Revelation 14:8, MKJV)

God views the spiritual ways and concepts of false worship as spiritual fornication. God promises eternal life and the millennial rule of Jesus Christ. True faith is all about the hope of a future life if we repent, clean up our lives, and learn to live by Godly Commandments and principles.

This spiritual fulfilment of false worship was valid for the first application in ancient Babylon until it was destroyed. It was also valid for any rebuild attempts. Furthermore it is also valid today, where some churches in some countries fall for the lure of its false ways of worship, and it will be valid in the "End Time".

Messiah is expected to return to dispute the ways and misunderstandings of false churches and religions, which will have drifted into the exact falseness and fake religion that was practiced in Babylon in the beginning.

It does not have a specific time element but is a man-made false way of worship that can exist in world empires. It will be prevalent and even enforced in the Last Days. Messiah is shown to destroy it upon His return.

A day for a year principle

Sometimes, in prophecy, we see the day for a year principle. Notice the following example:

> "I've assigned you to sleep this way for 390 days, representing the years they've been sinning, as you bear symbolically the punishment of the house of Israel.
>
> When you have completed this, you are to sleep on your right side, symbolically bearing the iniquity of Judah for 40 days. **Each day** that I've assigned to you represents **one year**."
>
> (Ezekiel 4:5-6, MKJV) [Emphasis mine]

This is also the case for the prophecies of Jonah and the expanded meaning as it has bearing on Jesus' life.

Jonah preached for three days. After that, Nineveh had 40 days to repent or be destroyed. We have seen that Jesus preached for three years and was killed. After that,

Jerusalem had 40 years to repent or be destroyed. When the day for a year principle was fulfilled, as Jesus was crucified in 30/31 AD and Jerusalem was destroyed 40 years later, in 70 AD. It happened and the principle was proven.

A day for 50 years principle

In some rare occasions, we can see a day for a Jubilee principle. Notice the law concerning the Jubilee, the fiftieth year.

> "And you shall make the fiftieth year holy, one year, and proclaim liberty throughout the land to all its inhabitants. It shall be a Jubilee to you, and you shall return each man to his possession, and you shall return each man to his family.
>
> (Leviticus 25:10, MKJV)

In the Jubilee year, all enslaved people are set free. Labor contracts are cancelled. Debts are forgiven and cleared. Families return to their ancestral farms. It is a time of economic reset. There should not be multigenerational poverty in Israel, not under God's law. The land belongs to God, and Israelites were to deal mercifully with each other.

> "The land shall not be sold forever; for the land is Mine. For you are strangers and pilgrims with Me."
>
> (Leviticus 25:23, MKJV)

Israel, at times, neglected this law of Leviticus 25 and its precepts. When they neglected the Sabbath years, they lost sight of the Jubilee and did not implement it. It was something that some affluent families did not want to practice, and they presumably pressured the kings to abandon it. They even pushed for alternate laws so that the rich people would not have to allow the low-income families to regain ancestral land. They prevented the economic reset that God required every 50 years. At such times, affluent families also lost their inheritance when foreign powers invaded and captured them! That's why God allowed calamities to come. It was punishment on the elite for misusing their positions of power. In a sense, God then allowed a foreign power to enforce an economic reset on Israel.

> "And the ones who had escaped from the sword he carried away to Babylon, where they were servants to him and his sons until the reign of the kingdom of Persia,
>
> to fulfill the Word of Jehovah in the mouth of Jeremiah, until the land had enjoyed its sabbaths. All the days of the desolation it kept the sabbath, to the full measure of seventy years."
>
> (2 Chronicles 36:20-21, MKJV)

Historical records show that Israel had gone into slavery on more than one occasion because they neglected the land Sabbaths, which were to occur every seven years. In the process, then, the Jubilee was also ignored. Because of this, they would lose their inheritance.

"And I will scatter you among the nations, and will draw out a sword after you. And your land shall be waste, and your cities waste.

Then shall the land enjoy its sabbaths, as long as it lies waste, and you are in your enemies' land; then shall the land rest and enjoy its sabbaths.

As long as it lies waste it shall rest, because it did not rest in your sabbaths when you lived on it."

(Leviticus 26:33-35, MKJV)

This will happen, by extension, wherever Israel was banished to in the world. This was also the case in the dispersion to the area known today as Europe, which is to the north and west of Jerusalem. Later, the lost Ten Tribes of Israel migrated further when anti-Semitism forced them to migrate even further, and many settled in the British Isles. Ultimately, they even migrated further across the oceans into new worlds where they gained freedoms from central European oppression. It is a principle that is happening again. Remember this as we discover the countdown to the year 2030.

To understand the current world scene, we must consider observing a distinction between the following groups in prophecies:

1) Jews around Judea and elsewhere in the world.
2) The Lost Ten Tribes of Israel that lost their identity in the world.
3) Christians in the world striving to following Jesus Christ.

Identification of Jews

After the banishment of the Northern Kingdom consisting of the Ten Tribes of Israel, the Southern Kingdom still survived for a while. But when they made idols of stones and wood to fabricate alternate forms of worships, God also allowed them to be taken captive and migrated to foreign lands.

> "And I saw, when for all the causes for which backsliding Israel committed adultery, I sent her away and gave a bill of divorce to her, yet her treacherous sister Judah did not fear, but she went and whored, she also.
>
> And it happened, from the folly of her whoredom, she defiled the land and fornicated with stones and stocks.
>
> And yet for all this her treacherous sister Judah has not turned to Me with her whole heart, but with falsehood, says Jehovah.
>
> And Jehovah said to me, The backsliding Israel has justified herself more than treacherous Judah."
>
> (Jeremiah 3:8-11, MKJV)

Israel here refers to the Ten Tribes that initially settled in the northern part of the Promised Land. They were first allowed to go into slavery. Later, the other two tribes around Jerusalem and the south which is referred to as Judah in this scripture were also taken away.

During the restoration under Ezra and Nehemiah, as prophesied by Daniel, mainly two tribes returned: Judah and Levi. Judah settled in Judea, and Levi restarted and performed the Temple services. There was also a remnant of the tribe of Benjamin involved. They were collectively called Jews.

Identification of Israel

After the restoration under Ezra and Nehemiah, the northern section of the Promised Land was still occupied by migrants from other nations. They were called Samarians. Jesus visited them during His ministry.

"A woman of Samaria came to draw water. Jesus said to her, Give me to drink.

(For His disciples had gone away into the city to buy food.)

Then the woman of Samaria said to Him, How do you, being a Jew, ask a drink of me, who am a woman of Samaria? For the Jews do not associate with Samaritans."

(John 4:7-9, MKJV)

The Lost Ten Tribes of Israel did not return and mostly stayed in suburbs of cities in gentile countries where they were taken to by gentile kings in the past.

Jesus mainly preached in and around Judea. The prophecies of Jerusalem applied initially to the Jews of Judea. That was His mission.

Jesus sent His 12 disciples to the Lost Ten Tribes of Israel in the suburbs of nearby surrounding countries.

"Jesus sent out these twelve, commanding them, saying, Do not go into the way of the nations, and do not enter into any city of the Samaritans.

But rather go to the lost sheep of the house of Israel."

(Matthew 10:5-6, MKJV)

These Lost Ten Tribes migrated north and west towards France, Spain and Portugal, then the British Isles, and ultimately across the oceans. They will be adversely affected by this prophecy of the End Time events.

Identification of Christians

From the preaching and ministry of Jesus Christ and later His Apostles, and in particular the Apostle Paul, Christians became converted. Some Christians originally were circumcised Jews in Judea and, by extension, also circumcised Israelites evangelized from Jewish synagogues in surrounding countries. The Disciples went throughout the Roman Empire, as far as Greece and even the Isles of Britain. They also went south into Egypt and

East towards India. Gentiles who visited Synagogues and sat in the side courts converted to Christianity and were baptized.

> "And the Jews having gone out of the synagogue, the nations begged that these words might be preached to them the next sabbath.
>
> And the synagogue being broken up, many of the Jews and of the devout proselytes followed Paul and Barnabas; who, speaking to them, persuaded them to continue in the grace of God.
>
> And on the coming sabbath day almost all the city came together to hear the Word of God."
>
> (Acts 13:42-44, MKJV)

Therefore in the rest of this book, a distinction will be made between Jews, the Lost Ten Tribes (generally English speaking), and Christians in general. The prophecies and timescales differ between these three groups.

Chapter 2

Prophecies Revealed

A closer examination of the events of Jonah's ministry is necessary, as these events serve as prophetic indicators of Jesus' ministry and hold significance for both Israel and Christianity in the Last Days. This analysis contributes to understanding the importance of 2030.

An excerpt from the book "The Sign of Jonah – expanded" will be included to elucidate why 2030 is regarded as a significant year in prophecy.

Jonah served as a prophet during the reign of the kings of Israel. Although many readers of the Bible may not recall him as a prominent prophet who shaped Israel's history, his contributions were significant. He exerted influence over the monarchy, as evidenced by his mention in the Book of Kings:

"He restored the border of Israel from the entering of Hamath to the sea of the plain, according to the Word of Jehovah, the God of Israel, which He spoke by the hand of his servant **Jonah**, the son of Amittai, the prophet, who was from Gath-hepher."
(2 Kings 14:25, MKJV)

Jonah prophesied in Jerusalem prior to his mission to Nineveh. While the Book of Jonah focuses exclusively on Nineveh, additional aspects of his prophetic ministry are evident in other texts. His prophecies were fulfilled and had enduring consequences, reflecting the will of God. These events should be regarded as highly significant by believers.

A pivotal event was about to occur in Jonah's life. The narrative continues at the outset of the Book of Jonah.

> "And the Word of Jehovah came to Jonah
> the son of Amittai, saying,
> Arise, go to Nineveh, that great city, and
> cry against it; for their evil has come up
> before Me."
> (Jonah 1:1-2, MKJV)

Previously, Jonah delivered messages to the kings of Jerusalem; now, he was tasked with delivering a message to Nineveh, a city considered an enemy of Israel.

> "But Jonah rose up to flee to Tarshish
> from the presence of Jehovah. And he
> went down to Joppa. And he found a
> ship going to Tarshish. And he gave its
> fare, and went down into it, in order to go
> with them to Tarshish, away from the
> sight of Jehovah."
> (Jonah 1:3, MKJV)

Jonah's decision to flee from his divine assignment may appear unusual. The reasons for his actions will be explored subsequently. Nevertheless, God's purposes prevailed, compelling Jonah to fulfill his mission. God's concern extends beyond Israel to all humanity, as demonstrated by the opportunity given to

Nineveh to repent before facing destruction. The following narrative illustrates how Jonah was compelled to obey.

"But Jehovah hurled a great wind into the sea, and there was a great storm in the sea, so that the ship was thought to be broken.

Then the seamen were afraid, and each man cried to his god. And they threw out the ship's articles in the ship, into the sea in order to lighten it. But Jonah had gone down into the hold of the ship; and he lay there, and was fast asleep.

And the chief of the seaman came to him and said to him, What is it to you, O sound sleeper? Arise, call upon your God! It may be that our god will notice us, and we will not perish.

And they said, each one to his fellow, Come and let us cast lots, so that we may know who has caused this evil to occur to us. And they cast lots, and the lot fell on Jonah.

Then they said to him, Please tell us, for what reason this evil has come on us. What is your business? And where do you come from? Where is your country? And of what people are you?

And he said to them, I am a Hebrew; and I fear Jehovah, the God of heaven, who has made the sea and the dry land.

Then the men were afraid with a great fear. And they said to him, What is this you have done? For the men knew that he was fleeing from before the face of Jehovah, because he had told them." (Jonah 1:4-10, MKJV)

With the truth revealed, all those present understood the situation. Jonah recognized the gravity of his actions and perceived self-sacrifice as the only solution.

"Then they said to him, What shall we do to you, that the sea may be calm to us? For the sea was going on and being stormy.
And he said to them, Take me up and throw me out into the sea. And the sea shall be calm to you; for I know that this great storm has come on you for my sake.
But the men rowed hard to bring it to the land; but they could not, for the sea was going on and being stormy against them.
And they cried to Jehovah and said, We beg You, O Jehovah, we beg You, let us not perish for this man's life, and do not lay on us innocent blood. For You, O Jehovah, have done as it pleased You.
And they lifted Jonah up and threw him out into the sea; and the sea ceased from its raging."
(Jonah 1:11-15, MKJV)

At this juncture, the sailors recognized the significance of Jonah's identity. Although Jonah believed death was inevitable, God continued to provide opportunities and perform miracles. The subsequent events had a profound impact on the sailors, leading to their repentance.

> "Then the men feared Jehovah
> exceedingly, and offered a sacrifice to
> Jehovah, and vowed vows.
> And Jehovah had prepared a great fish to
> swallow up Jonah. And Jonah was in the
> belly of the fish three days and three
> nights."
> (Jonah 1:16-17, MKJV)

Jonah's experience prefigured the sacrificial death of Jesus Christ at the crucifixion. It prompted sincere repentance among both Jews and Gentiles. Jesus referenced this event during his earthly ministry, as recorded in the Gospels, thereby broadening the scope of Jonah's prophecies. The narrative continues with the miracle of Jonah's deliverance from the fish and his profound repentance.

> "And Jonah prayed to Jehovah his God
> out of the fish's belly,
> and he said, I cried to Jehovah from my
> distress. And He answered me. Out of the
> belly of Sheol I cried for help, and You
> heard my voice.
> For You cast me into the depths of the
> seas, and the current surrounded me. All
> Your breakers and Your waves passed
> over me.

Then I said, I am cast off from Your eyes,
yet I will look again toward Your holy
temple.
Waters encompassed me, even to the
soul; the depth closed around me; the
seaweed was bound to my head.
I went down to the bottoms of the
mountains; the earth with her bars was
around me forever; yet You have brought
up my life from the pit, O Jehovah my
God.
When my soul fainted within me, I
remembered Jehovah; and my prayer
came in to You, into Your holy temple.
They who take heed to lying vanities
forsake their kindness;
but I will sacrifice to You with the voice of
thanksgiving; I will fulfill that which I
have vowed. Salvation belongs to
Jehovah!"
(Jonah 2:1-9, MKJV)

Following Jonah's sincere and desperate
repentance, God granted him another opportunity.
Similarly, Nineveh was given a chance to avoid
destruction, which had previously seemed inevitable.
God's intention was to intervene and prevent disaster.

"And Jehovah spoke to the fish, and it
vomited Jonah out on the dry land."
Jonah 2:10, MKJV)

From a naturalistic perspective, it is plausible that
a large air-breathing fish experiencing distress might

beach itself to survive. Jonah's protection from the fish's stomach acids and subsequent expulsion onto the shore would have been a remarkable event. This occurrence held particular significance for the people of Nineveh, some of whom practiced pagan beliefs, including the worship of large sea creatures. Witnessing Jonah emerge from the fish would likely have inspired awe and facilitated the rapid spread of his story throughout the community. Jonah expected the people to turn from their pagan practices and worship the Creator, who demonstrated authority over creation.

> "And the Word of Jehovah came to Jonah the second time, saying,
> Arise, go to Nineveh, that great city, and cry out to it the proclamation that I am declaring to you.
> And Jonah arose and went to Nineveh, according to the Word of Jehovah. And Nineveh was a very great city of **three days'** journey.
> And Jonah began to enter into the city a day's journey, and he cried and said, Yet **forty days** and Nineveh shall be overthrown!"
> (Jonah 3:1-4, MKJV) [emphasis mine]

The numbers **three** and forty are symbolically significant. Three often represents completeness, while forty signifies a period of trial and testing that may result in repentance. The significance of these numbers will be explored in subsequent chapters.

It is important to note the sequence: **three days** of walking and preaching, followed by forty days allotted for repentance before impending disaster. This sequence will be explained in detail in the next chapter.

Chapter 3

Time Sequences Revealed

Despite three years of Jesus' ministry and miracles in Judea, many individuals continued to seek a sign from Christ to confirm His identity as the Son of God, as referenced in Matthew 12:38.

"Then some of the scribes and Pharisees said to him, "Teacher, we wish to see a sign from you."
But he answered them, "An evil and adulterous generation seeks for a sign; but no sign shall be given to it except the sign of the prophet Jonah."
(Matthew 12:38 - 39, RSV)

Christ warned the unbelieving scribes, Pharisees, and Sadducees that no further public sign would be provided except the Sign of Jonah. To understand the nature of this sign, we examine the following verse.

"For as Jonah was three days and three nights in the belly of the whale, so will the Son of man be three days and three nights in the heart of the earth."
(Matthew 12:40, RSV)

At first glance, the Sign appears to refer solely to Christ being in the tomb for three days and three nights before His resurrection. However, additional dimensions exist. We will examine Jonah's experiences and ministry in Nineveh to gather further details, then apply these insights to the events in Jerusalem and consider their relevance to contemporary contexts.

We will now analyze the timeline of Jonah's ministry and compare it with the chronology of Christ's ministry.

A day for a year

Two significant time elements are present: Jonah preached for three days, and Nineveh was given forty days to repent or face destruction. A potential parallel may exist between the events involving Jonah and those concerning Christ.

Applying the day-for-a-year principle reveals that the Sign of Jonah conveyed a deeper message to the Pharisees and the Jerusalem priesthood.

It is widely recognized that Christ preached in Judea for three years before being crucified in the fourth year (31 AD), as the Gospel accounts establish.

The following comparison is noteworthy:

Jonah preached for three days, while Christ preached for three years. The question arises regarding the forty days granted to Nineveh for repentance: did a similar period apply to Jerusalem?

It is widely accepted that Christ was crucified during the fourth year of His ministry, having preached from 27 AD to 30 AD and subsequently crucified in 31 AD. Jerusalem was destroyed forty years later, in 70 AD. This sequence aligns with the Sign of Jonah when interpreted through the prophetic day-for-a-year principle.

Jonah preached for three days, corresponding to Christ's three years of ministry. Similarly, Nineveh was given forty days to repent, while Jerusalem was allotted forty years.

Nineveh repented within the allotted forty days and was spared, whereas Jerusalem did not repent during its forty-year period and was ultimately destroyed by the Roman army.

These observations represent the broader implications of the Sign of Jonah as prophesied by Jesus Christ. This interpretation contributes to understanding Christ's discussion with the Pharisees in Matthew 12.

> "41 The men of Nineveh will arise at the judgment with this generation and condemn it; for they repented at the preaching of Jonah, and behold, something greater than Jonah is here." (Matthew 12:41, RSV)

When Christ presented the sign of Jonah to the Pharisees, He was not solely referring to His time in the tomb. He was also conveying to the people and the priesthood of Jerusalem that, after three years of preaching, they would have forty years to repent or risk losing their inheritance in the Promised Land and face the destruction of Jerusalem. This interpretation holds considerable significance.

Apostle's 40 days of repentance

Following the fulfillment of the Sign of Jonah, in which Jesus remained in the tomb for three days and three nights, He was resurrected and continued to instruct His disciples. The resurrection occurred after Passover, during the Feast of Unleavened Bread. From this point, the Israelites were instructed to count fifty days to Pentecost. During this period, the Apostles engaged in forty days of preparation and repentance to equip themselves for their mission to spread the Gospel.

Understanding this sequence requires familiarity with the Mosaic Law observed by Jesus and His apostles. The relevant instructions are outlined in Leviticus:

> "And you shall count to you from the next day after the sabbath, from the day that you brought the sheaf of the wave offering; seven sabbaths shall be complete.
> To the next day after the seventh sabbath you shall number fifty days. And you shall offer a new food offering to Jehovah."
> (Leviticus 23:15-16, MKJV)

Jesus was resurrected after nightfall at the beginning of the Sabbath. On the following day, He ascended to the third Heaven to serve as the Wave Sheaf offering, presented to God as the first and perfect example of what would be gathered through the ministry of the twelve apostles. The events of this initial Sabbath are as follows:

> "The **first of the sabbaths** Mary Magdalene came early to the tomb, darkness still being on it, and she saw the stone taken away from the tomb" (John 20:1, MKJV) [Emphasis mine]

Later that day, Jesus appeared to Mary prior to His presentation to God during the Ascension. He remained untouched by humans, maintaining ritual purity as required of the High Priest.

> "Jesus said to her, Do not touch Me, for I have not yet ascended to My Father. But go to My brothers and say to them, I ascend to My Father and Your Father, and to My God and your God." (John 20:17, MKJV)

The following events then transpired.

Beginning on the first day after the weekly Sabbath, when the women discovered that Jesus had already risen, the counting of seven weeks commenced in accordance with the Law in Leviticus. This period, culminating in the fiftieth day known as Pentecost, marked the start of the weeks or Sabbaths as prescribed in Leviticus 23.

> "¶ Then the same day at evening, being the first day of the sabbaths, when the doors were shut where the disciples were assembled for fear of the Jews, Jesus

came and stood in the midst, and said to
them, Peace to you!"
(John20:19, MKJV)

After Jesus ascended and was presented to God as
the perfect High Priest, He could then be physically
touched.

"And when He had said this, He showed
them His hands and His side. Then the
disciples were glad when they saw the
Lord."
(John 20:20, MKJV)

Subsequently, the incident occurred in which
Thomas, often referred to as 'doubting Thomas,' was
permitted to physically touch Jesus.

"Then He said to Thomas, Reach your
finger here and behold My hands; and
reach your hand here and thrust it into
My side; and do not be unbelieving, but
believing."
(John 20:27, MKJV)

This event took place during the second week
following Jesus' resurrection. Additional events occurred,
during which Jesus repeatedly tested the disciples,
expecting further repentance. This process continued for
forty days:

"¶ Truly, O Theophilus, I made the first
report as to all things that Jesus began
both to do and teach

until the day He was taken up, having given directions to the apostles whom He chose, through the Holy Spirit;
to whom He also presented Himself living after His suffering by many infallible proofs, being seen by them through **forty days**, and speaking of the things pertaining to the kingdom of God."
(Acts 1:1-3, MKJV) [Emphasis mine]

It is possible that the message was intended for the disciples, indicating that a period of forty days of final repentance was necessary before receiving the Holy Spirit and becoming fully commissioned Apostles on the fiftieth day, Pentecost.

Another parallel can be observed in the biblical text: from the Sabbath during the Feast of Unleavened Bread, seven Sabbaths are counted, and the day following this period, the fiftieth day, is Pentecost.
The Jubilee is also counted by keeping seven land Sabbaths, and then the fiftieth year is the Jubilee. Compare the following scriptures:

"And you shall number seven sabbaths of years to you, seven times seven years.
And the time of the seven sabbaths of years shall be forty-nine years to you.
Then you shall cause the trumpet of the jubilee to sound on the tenth of the seventh month; in the day of atonement, the trumpet shall sound throughout all your land.
And you shall make the fiftieth year holy, one year, and proclaim liberty

> throughout the land to all its
> inhabitants. It shall be a jubilee to you,
> and you shall return each man to his
> possession, and you shall return each
> man to his family."
> (Leviticus 25:8-10, MKJV)

Compare the 50 years of the Jubilee to the 50 days to Pentecost:

> "And you shall count to you from the
> next day after the sabbath, from the day
> that you brought the sheaf of the wave
> offering; seven sabbaths shall be
> complete.
> To the next day after the seventh sabbath
> you shall number fifty days. And you
> shall offer a new food offering to
> Jehovah."
> (Leviticus 23:15-16, MKJV)

Thus, the fiftieth day was designated as a Sabbath day, just as the fiftieth year was observed as a Sabbath year. This illustrates the recurring principle of the number fifty in biblical tradition.

On the day of Pentecost, the Holy Spirit descended upon the disciples, empowering them to serve as fully commissioned Apostles.

> "And in the fulfilling of the day of
> Pentecost, they were all with one accord
> in one place.
> And suddenly a sound came out of the
> heaven as borne along by the rushing of

a mighty wind, and it filled all the house
where they were sitting.
And tongues as of fire appeared to them,
being distributed; and it sat upon each of
them.
And they were all filled of the Holy Spirit,
and began to speak in other languages,
as the Spirit gave them utterance."
(Acts 2:1-4, MKJV)

Jesus indicated that this occasion would hold significant importance.

"And the book of the prophet Isaiah was
handed to Him. And unrolling the book,
He found the place where it was written,
"The Spirit of the Lord is on Me; because
of this He has anointed Me to proclaim
the Gospel to the poor. He has sent me to
heal the brokenhearted, to proclaim
deliverance to the captives, and new
sight to the blind, to set at liberty those
having been crushed,
to proclaim the acceptable year of the
Lord.""
(Luke 4:17-19, MKJV)

The fiftieth year, known as the Jubilee, has historically been regarded as a period of release from debt, past difficulties, and even the consequences of sin. This time often provided the next generation with freedom from previous mistakes, breaking cycles of poverty. The intended purpose was for governing authorities to facilitate this release rather than to favor the wealthy. Failure to observe these principles could result in adverse consequences for the government and those in positions of power.

A day for a Jubilee

A Jubilee occurs every 50 years according to the biblical calendar and established time cycles.

It is important to note that primarily the tribes of Judah, Levi, and a portion of Benjamin returned after the earlier exile and were present during the ministry of Jesus Christ. These groups were given a period of 40 years following the crucifixion to repent or risk losing their inheritance.

The fate of the other ten lost tribes, who were dispersed throughout Greece and the broader Roman Empire, remains a subject of inquiry.

Applying the 'day for a Jubilee' principle, 40 days (as referenced in the warning to Nineveh) multiplied by 50 years (the length of a Jubilee) results in a period of 2,000 years following the crucifixion. This duration is interpreted as the time allotted for the Lost Ten Tribes, dispersed throughout the Roman Empire and beyond, to repent and return to adherence to God's commandments; otherwise, they risk forfeiting their inheritance in suburbs in other countries, as gracefully empowerd by God .

Calculating from the crucifixion, traditionally dated to 30 or 31 AD, this period concludes in the year 2030 AD. Further evidence supporting this interpretation is presented below.

It is essential to understand the extent of the dispersion of the Lost Ten Tribes to which this prophecy refers.

The tribe of Nathan is generally believed to have settled in Scotland, particularly among the royal lineage. Additional information is provided in the reference below.

The Line of Nathan

(https://www.ucg.org/bible-study-tools/ebooklet/the-throne-of-britain/appendix-11-joseph-of-arimathea-and-the-line-of)

Joseph of Arimathea, who bought the Body of Jesus after the crucifixion, had connections with the royalty in Scotland. See the link below:

Joseph of Arimathea

(https://www.bbc.co.uk/thepassion/articles/joseph_of_ari mathea.shtml)

In the King's Acre grave yard in Scotland is a tombstone with the following inscription:

"HERE LIES THE BODY OF THAT MOST NOBLE DISCIPLE, RECORDED IN SCRIPTURE BY THE NAME OF JOSEPH OF ARIMATHEA, AND NOTED BY THE FOUR EVANGELISTS, ST. MATTHEW, MARK, LUKE, AND JOHN, FOR HIS BEGGING THE BODY OF OUR BLESSED SAVIOUR WHEN CRUCIFIED TO REDEEM LOST MEN FROM ETERNAL DESTRUCTION, AND BURYING IT IN A TOMB OF HIS OWN MAKING. HE DIED A.D. 45, AGED 86."

Tombstone of Joseph of Arimathea

(https://d.lib.rochester.edu/camelot/text/history-of-that-holy-disciple-joseph-of-arimathea)

After the 1600s, the so-called Lost Tribes of Israel migrated to regions including the United States and other British colonies such as Australia and New Zealand. These groups subsequently accumulated significant wealth and influence, which some interpret as the fulfillment of promises made to Abraham in later periods. However, it is argued that these societies have increasingly neglected their Christian heritage, as evidenced by the removal of Christianity from educational institutions. Some perspectives suggest that this shift may result in the eventual loss of their inheritance, prosperity, and influence in the eschatological 'Last Days.' The rise of religious pluralism and the increasing influence of groups with values perceived as contrary to traditional Christianity are often cited as contributing factors to this decline.

See the book on the Nations of the Last Days.

(https://www.amazon.com/gp/product/B08DTHBJD4?ref_=dbs_m_mng_rwt_calw_tkin_3&storeType=ebooks)

Additional transgressions and factors contributing to the loss of inheritance by the Lost Ten Tribes from 2030 onward will be discussed in subsequent chapters.

First, we will examine the historical impact of the Jubilee cycle. Although leaders in Israel may have reasons for not implementing the Jubilee cycle in

Jerusalem and the land of Israel, this does not preclude the unfolding of divine temporal sequences in the future.

The Lost Ten Tribes may be unaware of their obligation to observe the Jubilee system and implement land Sabbaths; however, this lack of awareness is inconsequential. The overuse and mismanagement of farmlands will result in soil degradation and dust bowl conditions, leading to significant consequences. The prophetic implications of the Jubilee cycle will persist, and the year 2030 will mark the onset of substantial changes.

> "You shall not do these so that the land
> may not spew you out also when you
> defile it, as it spewed out the nations that
> were before you."
> (Leviticus 18:28, MKJV)

In the following chapter, we will analyze the effects of the 50-year cycles on Jews residing in the land of Israel, as well as on the Lost Ten Tribes dispersed to the so-called "free lands."

Chapter 4

Signs of the Time

Numerous indicators suggest that the Jubilee cycle continues to influence events, particularly for Jewish communities in Israel and for the so-called Lost Ten Tribes of Israel residing in countries such as the United States, Britain, Australia, and New Zealand. The following examples illustrate this ongoing phenomenon.

Historical records indicate that the Turks assumed control over Israel and Jerusalem in 1517. Precisely eight Jubilee cycles later, in 1917, during World War I, the British army liberated Israel and Jerusalem, facilitating the reestablishment of a Jewish state. The issuance of the Balfour Declaration marked the return of the Promised Land to the Jewish people. Fifty years later, in 1967, Jerusalem was formally and legally integrated with the rest of Israel following the Six-Day War. During this conflict, the Israeli army achieved a decisive victory over several Arab nations within six days, without engaging in combat on either Sabbath. This event occurred exactly nine Jubilee cycles after the initial Turkish conquest of Jerusalem in 1517. See the links below:

(https://www.jewishvirtuallibrary.org/ottoman-rule-1517-1917)

Balfour Declaration

(https://www.britannica.com/event/Balfour-Declaration)

The United States played a significant role in establishing a constitution and government that guaranteed freedom of religion. Additionally, the United States has supported the Jewish population in the Promised Land, contributing to their security and survival within a frequently adversarial regional context. Some scholars suggest that the founding and historical trajectory of the United States align with the Jubilee cycle.

In 1620, the Mayflower transported approximately 40 members of a Puritan Christian congregation among its 100 passengers. These Puritan settlers are often regarded as foundational figures in American history, as their advocacy contributed to the inclusion of human rights and religious freedom in the American Constitution. This foundation enabled the United States to develop into a global power with the capacity to support and protect Israel.

See the link below:

The Mayflower journey

(https://www.history.com/topics/colonial-america/mayflower)

Exactly 400 years later, corresponding to eight **Jubilees**, during a global pandemic originating in China, the 2020 United States presidential election was reportedly decided by the inclusion of ballot papers counted several days after the official voting day. Subsequently, a new administration succeeded a previous leader who had recognized Jerusalem as the capital of

Israel, a decision that elicited significant concern in the Arab world.

Since 2020, there has been a perception of increasing marginalization of Christianity in the United States, particularly under the Biden administration. Other faiths are afforded equal or, at times, greater influence within educational and institutional settings. Additionally, advocates for LGBTQ rights have gained influence in matters traditionally overseen by Christian leaders. These developments are interpreted by some as indicative of the arrival of the Last Days.

This decline is seen as undermining support for Israel and contributing to domestic challenges such as inflation, crime, and societal instability. The year 2020 is viewed by some as a potential turning point in American history, occurring 400 years after the initial reference point of eight **Jubilees**.

It is argued that the cycles of the Jubilee continue to exert influence, analogous to waves or ripples following a significant disturbance. The rejection and crucifixion of Jesus in Jerusalem are considered to have ongoing spiritual and political consequences, potentially extending into the present era and approaching 2030. These patterns warrant careful consideration.

The prophecies of Micah are regarded as relevant in the current context. Corruption and injustice are prevalent among societal elites, which historically have contributed to the decline of powerful nations. Such patterns are considered likely to recur.

"And I said, Please hear, O heads of
Jacob and magistrates of the house of
Israel. Is it not for you to know justice?

You who hate the good and love the evil;
who pull their skin off them, and their
flesh from their bones;
who also eat the flesh of My people, and
strip their skin off them. And they break
their bones and chop them in pieces, like
that in the pot, like those in the middle of
the kettle.
Then they shall cry to Jehovah, but He
will not answer them. He will even hide
His face from them at that time, as they
have done evil in their doings.
So says Jehovah concerning the prophets
who make My people err, who bite with
their teeth and cry, Peace! And whoever
does not give for their mouth, they even
sanctify a war against him."
(Micah 3:1-5, MKJV)

When a perceived spiritual conflict targets Christianity, Biblical teachings are removed from educational institutions, and religious leaders face legal and social pressures for refusing to conduct same-sex marriage ceremonies in Christian churches. Such developments are interpreted as contributing to the decline in national stability and security.

When moral values are inverted, and student activism opposes Biblical teachings, and secular perspectives are prioritized over religious doctrine, these trends are interpreted as indicative of a spiritual conflict. Such conditions are believed to result in a loss of national direction and guidance.

"Therefore a night shall be to you without vision; and darkness without divining.
And the sun shall go down over the prophets, and the day shall be dark over them.
And the seers shall be ashamed, and the diviners ashamed; yea, they shall all cover their mustache, for there is no answer from God.
But I am full of power by the Spirit of Jehovah, and justice, and might, to declare to Jacob his transgression, and to Israel his sin.
Please hear this, heads of the house of Jacob, and magistrates of the house of Israel, who hate justice and pervert all equity."
(Micah 3:6-9, MKJV)

Reliance on military force or the enforcement of laws that disproportionately benefit elites is unlikely to resolve underlying societal issues. Such approaches may exacerbate existing problems.

"They build up Zion with blood, and Jerusalem with iniquity.
Her heads judge for a bribe, and her priests teach for pay, and her prophets divine for silver, yet they will lean on Jehovah and say, Is not Jehovah among us? No evil can come on us!
Therefore, on account of you, Zion shall be plowed as a field, and Jerusalem shall

become heaps, and the mountain of the house into high places of the forest." (Micah 3:10-12, MKJV)

Ultimately, a transformation is anticipated upon the return of the Messiah, as described in the Book of Revelation. This outcome is presented as a divine promise.

"But it shall be in the last days the mountain of the house of Jehovah shall be established in the top of the mountains, and it shall be lifted up above the hills; and peoples shall flow to it.
And many nations shall come and say, Come and let us go up to the mountain of Jehovah, and to the house of the God of Jacob. And He will teach us of His ways, and we will walk in His paths; for the Law shall go forth out of Zion, and the Word of Jehovah from Jerusalem. And He shall judge between many peoples, and will decide for strong nations afar off; and they shall beat their swords into plowshares, and their spears into pruning hooks. Nation shall not lift up a sword against nation, And they shall not still learn war." (Micah 4:1-3, MKJV)

Until that time, the nation supporting Israel is expected to experience a decline, which may also affect the security of Jerusalem.

According to Christian doctrine, God initiated His Son's ministry in Judea nearly 2000 years ago.

"And you, Bethlehem Ephratah, you being least among the thousands of Judah, out of you He shall come forth to Me, to become Ruler in Israel, He whose goings forth have been from of old, from the days of eternity."
(Micah 5:2, MKJV)

However, the Messiah's ministry was ended after three and a half years through crucifixion, an event regarded as a significant miscarriage of justice by the political authorities of that era. Jesus Christ did not assume rulership over the nations from Jerusalem during His first advent. Consequently, humanity is believed to continue seeking salvation independently from Biblical guidance until its efforts ultimately prove unsuccessful.

"Therefore He will give them over until the time the one giving birth has given birth; then the rest of His brothers shall return to the sons of Israel."
(Micah 5:3, MKJV)

Israel was prophesied to lose its inheritance in the Promised Land.

After 40 years from the crucifixion, Jerusalem and even the Temple were destroyed in 70 AD. The Israelites were scattered again and migrated north and east, and eventually west, throughout Europe, even to the British Isles. At the right time, they went even further west to their "free nations" or states.

The Lost Ten Tribes were dispersed among various nations and are expected to remain so until the Last Days. Initially, these tribes are anticipated to achieve dominance over their adversaries while residing in their respective 'free worlds.'

> "And the remnant of Jacob shall be among the nations, in the midst of many peoples, like a lion among the beasts of the forest, like a young lion among the flocks of sheep, who, if he goes through, both tramples and tears in pieces. And there is none to snatch back.
> Your hand shall be high above your foes, and all your enemies shall be cut off."
> (Micah 5:8-9, MKJV)

However, as a result of sin and the veneration of human-made creations rather than God, these groups are expected to lose their strength through unforeseen circumstances.

> "And it shall be in that day, says Jehovah, I will cut off your horses out of your midst, and I will destroy your chariots.
> And I will cut off the cities of your land, and throw down all your strongholds.
> And I will cut off sorceries out of your hand, and there shall not be fortune-tellers among you.
> I will also cut off your graven images, and your pillars out of the midst of you; and

you shall never again worship the work
of your hands."
(Micah 5:10, 13, MKJV)

It is believed that God will permit weakness to affect the great nation, providing an opportunity to address the Lost Ten Tribes of Israel as well as the Jewish people in Israel, and to ultimately present His case to Jerusalem at the Second Advent.

"Mountains, hear Jehovah's case, and
the constant foundations of the earth.
For Jehovah has a quarrel with His
people, and He will plead His case with
Israel."
(Micah 6:2, MKJV)

In the period approaching the End Times, it is anticipated that God will permit the dispersed people of Israel to experience adversity, prompting introspection and renewed engagement with scripture in preparation for the Second Coming of the Messiah. At that point, they will be receptive to His message.

However, some of the current leaders are not seeking God's wisdom in their decisions. The Bible is currently being banned from schools. Pastors are intimidated by rulers and courts. The Sodomite agenda is being forced onto Christian pastors. Evangelists are being jailed. Churches are being vandalized. Christianity is being trampled on.

Repentance by municipal leaders may avert the fulfillment of prophecy, as exemplified by the city of Nineveh. However, continued oppression of Christianity by competing ideologies is believed to permit the progression of prophecy, potentially resulting in the decline of Western 'Christian' cities.

Chapter 5

Rising Powers

By 2030 and in subsequent years, it is anticipated that other nations will surpass the so-called "free worlds" in influence. The Lost Ten Tribes, dispersed throughout the Western world and associated with a diluted and syncretized form of Christianity, are projected to experience a decline in both prominence and security. In this context, authoritarian regimes and alternative religious groups are expected to gain increased power over these populations.

Throughout history, multiple nations have posed significant threats to the existence of Israel. These entities have endangered Jerusalem and inflicted considerable harm upon the inhabitants and property within the Promised Land. According to biblical accounts, a similar situation is anticipated during the end times.

Gog and Magog

The nations of Gog and Magog have periodically posed significant threats to the people and cities of Israel. According to biblical accounts, these groups originated from the post-Flood dispersion of Noah's descendants and subsequently migrated eastward from the region surrounding Mount Ararat.

> "Now these are the generations of the
> sons of Noah, Shem, Ham, and Japheth.
> And sons were born to them after the
> flood.
> The sons of Japheth: Gomer and **Magog**
> and Madai and Javan and Tubal and
> Meshech and Tiras."
> (Genesis 10:1-2, MKJV) [Emphasis mine]

Numerous biblical scholars have identified Gog and Magog with regions in the Far East, specifically associating them with China, Mongolia, and Russia. The historical record of the Genghis Khan dynasty demonstrates the extensive influence and, at times, the violent conquests attributed to these groups. These campaigns extended into Europe and eventually southward, impacting the Promised Land through acts of aggression.

The prophet Ezekiel documented the actions of these nations throughout history, with particular emphasis on their roles in eschatological events.

> "And the Word of Jehovah came to me,
> saying,
> Son of man, set your face against Gog,
> the land of **Magog**, the chief ruler of
> Rosh, Meshech, and Tubal, and prophesy
> against him.
> And say, So says the Lord Jehovah:
> Behold, I am against you, O Gog, the
> chief ruler of Rosh, Meshech and Tubal.
> And I will turn you back, and put hooks
> into your jaws, and I will bring you out,

and all your army, horses and horsemen,
all of them clothed most perfectly, a great
assembly with buckler and shield, all of
them swordsmen;"
(Ezekiel 38:1-4, MKJV) [Emphasis mine]

According to the prophetic narrative, these nations are drawn into a major conflict in the eschatological period, relying on their military capabilities. However, the prophecy asserts that they will ultimately face destruction by divine intervention. It is suggested that they will form alliances with India (historically referred to as Persia) and certain African nations, a development some interpret as foreshadowed by the contemporary BRICS alliance.

"Persia, Ethiopia, and Libya with them,
all of them with shield and helmet;
Gomer and all his bands; the house of
Togarmah from the recesses of the north,
and all his bands; and many peoples
with you.
Be prepared; yea, prepare for yourself,
you and all your assembly that are
assembled to you, and be a guard to
them.
After many days you will be visited. In
the **latter years** you shall come into the
land turned back from the sword,
gathered out of many peoples, on the
mountains of Israel, which have always
been waste. (But he has been brought
out of the peoples, and they shall dwell
securely, all of them.)"
(Ezekiel 38:5-8, MKJV) [Emphasis mine]

Israel, along with the so-called Lost Ten Tribes residing in various autonomous states, is anticipated to experience periods of freedom and prosperity. This perceived overextension and liberal orientation may provoke hostility from Gog and Magog, who may interpret these societies as vulnerable and unprepared for large-scale conflict. However, such expectations are predicted to be ultimately unfulfilled.

It is proposed that these forces may first advance through Central Europe before moving southward toward Israel, an action that is prophesied to provoke divine retribution.

"And you shall come up on My people Israel like a cloud, to cover the land. It shall be in the last days, and I will bring you against My land, so that the nations may know Me when I shall be sanctified in you, O Gog, before their eyes."
(Ezekiel 38:16, MKJV)
A significant increase in the geopolitical influence of China, Russia, and India is anticipated, particularly after 2030.

The Kings of the North and South

The prophecies in the Book of Daniel depict a recurring confrontation over millennia between the King of the North and the King of the South. This pattern is expected to continue during the period known as the Last Days.

From Jerusalem's perspective, the King of the North is interpreted as the European Union, as any potential attack from the EU would approach from the north via the Mediterranean Sea. The King of the South is associated with the Arab alliance, which expanded into Egypt and North Africa and adopted Islam following the life of Mohammed, approximately 660 years after Christ.

Approximately 1,000 years ago, a confrontation between European states representing Christianity and the Muslim South led to the formation of the Crusaders, or Templars. These groups traveled from Europe to the south to engage in conflict with Muslim forces and to reclaim Jerusalem from the followers of Mohammed. Muslim forces had previously taken control of Jerusalem around 690 AD, and the Crusaders recaptured the city around 1079 AD. This historical sequence illustrates the persistent conflict between the King of the North and the King of the South.

Daniel chapter 11 offers an extensive discussion of these recurring confrontations, which are expected to persist into the Last Days. In recent history, European countries have permitted significant Muslim migration. However, many migrants have maintained their religious identity rather than assimilating into liberal European culture. This dynamic has been associated with social challenges, including increased crime rates and cultural tensions, which may contribute to further conflict and animosity.

> "And at the end-time, the king of the south shall butt at him. And the king of the north shall come against him like a tempest, with chariots and with horsemen and with many ships.
> And he shall enter into the countries and shall overflow and pass over. He shall

also enter into the glorious land, and many shall be stumbled. But these shall escape out of his hand: Edom and Moab, and the chief of the sons of Ammon."
(Daniel 11:40-41, MKJV)

The formation and consolidation of the European Union may present challenges to other nations, as its liberal cultural values, particularly those advocated by LGBTQ+ groups, could provoke opposition from various countries and religious communities. Efforts by these groups to gain influence in Africa and Muslim-majority countries may further intensify tensions. Additionally, the expansion of NATO is likely to increase military influence, which could provoke strong reactions from the Muslim South and regions in the Far East, often symbolized as Gog and Magog. As Europe seeks to reassert its influence over Africa, increased conflict and confrontation from the East are anticipated.

"But news out of the east and out of the north shall trouble him. Then he will go out with great fury to destroy, and to devote many to destruction."
(Daniel 11:44, MKJV)

It is anticipated that the European Union will increase in power and influence, potentially marginalizing other Western nations. Similarly, Muslim-majority countries are expected to gain greater influence. In response to perceived threats from the China-Russia-India axis, the EU may be compelled to strengthen and expand NATO.

Chapter 6

Changes are Coming

It is important to consider the anticipated changes leading up to 2030. These developments are projected to advance the world toward a scenario often described as the Last Days, culminating in a major global conflict. A war in Eastern Europe, initiated by forces from the Far East, is expected to unify Central Europe with financial support from Western Europe. As a result, NATO is likely to be strengthened. According to interpretations of Daniel's vision, the figure must have equally strong legs.

"This image's head was of fine gold; his breast and his arms were of silver; his belly and his thighs were of bronze;

his legs were of iron; his feet were part of iron and part of clay.

You watched until a stone was cut out without hands, which struck the image upon its feet which were of iron and clay, and broke them to pieces.

Then the iron, the clay, the bronze, the silver, and the gold were broken to pieces together. And they became like the chaff of the summer threshing floors. And the wind carried them away, so that no place was found for them. And the stone that struck the image became a great mountain and filled the whole earth."

(Daniel 2:32-35, MKJV)

According to this analysis, successive empires are expected to rise and fall until the second advent of the Messiah. The two 'legs' referenced are identified as Western and Central Europe. Between the present and 2030, it is anticipated that the Central European leg will be strengthened, analogous to an individual exercising both legs until they are equally capable of supporting him in battle. This development is projected to result in the formation of the entity known as the King of the North, as seen from Jerusalem. The impetus for this strengthening is expected to originate in the Far East and the Northeast, regions located east and north of Jerusalem.

"But news out of the east and out of the north shall trouble him."

(Daniel 11:44, MKJV)

NATO's expansion toward Russia and China is likely to meet resistance, as both states are expected to respond in various ways. India may also become involved, given its membership in the BRICS alliance. In the interim, increased activity by Russia and China may prompt political or social mobilization in Muslim-majority regions to the south, potentially prompting a northward movement toward Europe.

Although Europe may appear resilient, ongoing migration has been perceived by some as a challenge to traditional forms of Christianity. This demographic shift is viewed as contributing to cultural change, which may affect social cohesion during periods of conflict.

"And as to that which you saw: the feet and toes, part of potters' clay and part of iron; the kingdom shall be divided. But there shall be in it the strength of the iron, because you saw the iron mixed with miry clay. And as the toes of the feet were part of iron and part of clay, so the kingdom shall be partly strong and partly brittle. And as you saw iron mixed with miry clay, they shall mix themselves with the seed of men. But they shall not cling to one another, even as iron is not mixed with clay."

(Daniel 2:41-43, MKJV)

The European multicultural experiment may weaken the resolve to protect their nations in the end. Drastic measures may be taken.

The role of energy

Global energy demand continues to increase as technological advancements facilitate daily life. Economic activity and industrial production depend on electricity and machinery. Transportation systems, including cars, buses, trams, and trains, enable daily commutes, while international trade relies on business travel and the movement of goods by ships, trains, and trucks. However, these technologies contribute significantly to greenhouse gas emissions, driving global temperature rise.

Some interpretations of the Book of Revelation depict a future in which the sun scorches the earth, causing widespread devastation. Recent scientific observations suggest that rising global temperatures may reflect the onset of such scenarios, prompting significant concern among experts. Consequently, there is an urgent need to reduce reliance on fossil fuels.

"And men were burned with great heat. And they blasphemed the name of God, He having authority over these plagues. And they did not repent in order to give Him glory."

(Revelation 16:9, MKJV)

The transition away from fossil fuels raises significant concerns regarding the sustainability of current economic systems. Such a shift may fundamentally alter established ways of life and could create new dependencies, potentially leading to future conflicts. Furthermore, nations with differing ideologies or religious backgrounds may exploit these dependencies to exert power over others.

While Europe may attempt to reduce fossil fuel consumption, potentially at its own economic expense, it remains uncertain whether other major nations, such as China and India, will implement similar reductions.

Sanctions

A significant emerging trend is the increasing use of sanctions among nations. Disagreements over governmental practices and societal norms often lead to economic warfare, which can contribute to poverty and conflict.

When governments or authoritarian leaders misuse religion to justify oppression, they may be perceived as acting in a dehumanizing manner. These regimes often employ media and various other means to shape public opinion and behavior. The use of sanctions as a tool of oppression has been the subject of prophetic discourse.

"And there was given to it to give a spirit to the image of the beast, so that the image of the beast might both speak, and might cause as many as would not worship the image of the beast to be killed.

And it causes all, both small and great, rich and poor, free and bond, to receive a mark on their right hand, or in their foreheads,

even that not any might buy or sell except those having the mark, or the name of the beast, or the number of its name."

(Revelation 13:15-17, MKJV)

The religions of nations engaged in conflict are considered to be human constructs, as suggested by numerical symbolism. According to the Book of Genesis, humanity was granted the freedom to create both positive and negative outcomes, symbolized by the tree bearing both good and bad fruit. This choice prevented humanity from attaining everlasting fruit and eternal life. Negative actions can undermine and potentially destroy positive ones. It is posited that humanity was given six millennia to act according to its own will, after which the Messiah is expected to intervene to prevent self-destruction. The biblical narrative suggests that God permitted six days of human activity, requiring observance and reflection on the seventh day. The number "six" is interpreted as representing human effort, which ultimately fails to achieve lasting peace. The sequence "six six six" is viewed as a symbol of human endeavors that lack divine guidance, as outlined in the Bible, and are therefore destined to fail.

Ongoing sanctions are likely to destabilize global economies, foster animosity, and potentially escalate conflicts and destruction.

Weakening Western powers

The capacity of Western nations, particularly English-speaking countries (Lost Ten Tribes), to withstand emerging global powers in a shifting world order remains uncertain. The potential deployment of Western soldiers against authoritarian regimes raises questions regarding the primary beneficiaries of such interventions, including whether these actions are intended to protect millions of migrants from other countries.

The willingness of Christian conscripts to engage in conflicts against armies composed of individuals from different nations and religions is uncertain, particularly as Christianity faces challenges within their own societies.

Should urban environments become increasingly unsafe due to unaddressed crime, widespread unemployment, homelessness, hunger, and disease, the likelihood of soldiers participating in military engagements may be significantly affected.

If Christianity experiences oppression while other religions receive governmental support, the willingness of former soldiers to respond to military mobilization may be diminished. Furthermore, in contexts where moral decline is permitted, churches are harmed, Christians are marginalized, and justice is delayed, the authenticity and efficacy of parliamentary prayers, if any, may be called into question.

""They've sounded the alarm, and everyone is prepared, but no one is marching for battle, since I'm angry at the entire multitude.

The sword lurks outside, but pestilence and famine are on the prowl inside the house. Whoever is in the field will die by violence, while famine and pestilence will devour those in the city.

Fugitives will escape to the mountains like doves fleeing through the valleys, all of them moaning because of their own iniquity."

(Ezekiel 7:14-16, MKJV)

The willingness of soldiers to risk their lives for legislative decisions with which they may not personally agree raises questions about the motivations underlying national defense. Similarly, the extent to which families are prepared to make sacrifices for causes perceived as serving elite interests warrants examination. Technological advancements alone may be insufficient to ensure national security in the absence of collective resolve and a compelling rationale for defense. Furthermore, legal decisions that prioritize the rights of one group over another, such as cases involving religious and sexual minority rights, prompt debate regarding the broader societal and moral implications.

""Your country lies desolate; your cities have been incinerated. Before your very eyes, foreigners are devouring your land—they've brought devastation on it, while the land is overthrown by foreigners.

"The daughter of Zion is left abandoned, like a booth in a vineyard, like a hut in a cucumber field, or like a city under siege.

If the Lord of the Heavenly Armies hadn't left us a few survivors, we would be like Sodom; we would be like Gomorrah."

"Listen to what the LORD says, you rulers of Sodom, and pay attention to the teaching of our God, you people of Gomorrah!"

(Isaiah 1:7-10, MKJV)

The motivations driving soldiers from Western nations to engage in conflict remain a subject of debate. The question of whether divine support will be granted to them is also frequently discussed. Although Western leaders often enter into treaties and formal agreements, there remains uncertainty about whether authoritarian regimes will respect these commitments.

"For when they shall say, Peace and safety! Then sudden destruction comes on them, as travail upon a woman with child. And they shall not escape."

(1 Thessalonians 5:3, MKJV)

Authoritarian leaders could attempt to reclaim territories lost during the First and Second World Wars, potentially seeking to restore historical borders. This resurgence of historical nostalgia may coincide with a significant decline in Western influence and power after 2030. Some interpretations of Biblical prophecies suggest that such developments are anticipated. The broader implications of the warnings attributed to Jonah and Jesus Christ may therefore be realized.

Chapter 7

Towards the End

There will be wars and rumours of wars.

"And you will hear of wars and rumors of wars. See that you are not troubled, for all these things must occur; but the end is not yet.

For nation will rise against nation, and kingdom against kingdom. And there will be famines and pestilences and earthquakes in different places.

All these are the beginning of sorrows."

(Matthew 24:6-8, MKJV)

The period leading up to 2030 is expected to be marked by ongoing conflicts in multiple regions worldwide. These conflicts are primarily driven by ideological and religious differences. Such wars frequently result in further escalation and additional conflicts.

The horses run

The Book of Revelation depicts a recurring cycle of destruction. Within Christian theology, Jesus Christ is regarded as the only religious leader who sacrificed his life for humanity, enabling a deeper understanding of human sinfulness. The Crucifixion is the most significant miscarriage of justice, and is attributed to the Roman Empire, the Jewish Sanhedrin, and the Herodian dynasty, the ruling family in Jerusalem. According to Christian doctrine, Jesus demonstrated his divine royalty as the Son of God through supernatural means. He is uniquely positioned to distinguish authentic worship from false worship. Numerous forms of worship exist globally, many of which are considered inauthentic. Some scholars argue that Christianity itself was subject to infiltration and syncretism, resulting in elements of paganism and, to some extent, transforming it into a distorted form of religion. Christian tradition maintains that only Jesus is worthy to open the seals of the scroll that reveals humanity's failures, as he alone possesses perfect discernment of what is true to God and what is false.

> "And I saw when the Lamb opened one of the seals, and I heard one of the four living creatures like a sound of thunder, saying, Come and see.
>
> And I saw. And behold a white horse! And he sitting on it had a bow. And a crown was given to him, and he went forth conquering and to conquer."
>
> (Revelation 6:1-2, MKJV)

Leaders of certain religious movements have historically sought to compel adherence, sometimes resorting to force or collaborating with government authorities to enforce religious conformity. For example, during the Middle Ages in Europe, alliances between religious and political powers were common. In contrast, proponents of what is termed 'True Faith' assert that followers are gained through evangelism and are free to leave at any time.

Some religious groups acquire adherents through coercion, thereby restricting individuals' freedom to dissociate. Those who attempt to leave may face persecution. This phenomenon is sometimes symbolized by the 'first horse,' representing the proliferation of coercive religious movements.

Certain governments have been documented as manipulating or establishing religious systems to serve political objectives. In some cases, governmental ideologies may function as de facto religions, with individuals adopting these beliefs unconsciously.

An example often cited is the widespread acceptance of evolutionary theory, particularly macroevolution, in academic institutions. This theory posits that all life originated from a single-cell organism, with some hypotheses suggesting extraterrestrial origins for this cell. The process of increasing biological complexity, leading to the development of plants, animals, and eventually humans, is central to this framework. Critics argue that direct empirical evidence for these processes is lacking and that the supporting evidence is largely circumstantial. They contend that the acceptance of such theories has significant spiritual and societal implications.

Adherents to evolutionary theory are often characterized as rejecting belief in a divine Creator and attributing the complexity of life to natural processes. Critics assert that this worldview leads to existential pessimism and moral permissiveness, including the acceptance of practices such as abortion. These critiques are frequently framed within broader discussions about the societal impact of secular ideologies.

"And when He had opened the second seal, I heard the second living creature say, Come and see.

And another, a red horse, went out. And power was given to him sitting on it, to take peace from the earth, and that they should kill one another. And there was given to him a great sword."

(Revelation 6:3-4, MKJV)

Conflicts arising from ideological and religious differences often result in violence, crime, civil wars, and global conflicts. The subsequent destruction of infrastructure and livelihoods contributes to increased poverty and hunger.

"And when He had opened the third seal, I heard the third living creature say, Come and see. And I looked, and lo, a black horse. And he sitting on it had a balance in his hand.

And I heard a voice in the midst of the four living creatures say, A choenix of wheat for a denarius, and three choenixes of barley for a denarius. And do not hurt the oil and the wine."

(Revelation 6:5-6, MKJV)

The stress on human bodies and loss of health facilities then leads to sickness, disease, and pandemics.

> "And when He had opened the fourth seal, I heard the voice of the fourth living creature say, Come and see.

> And I looked, and behold, a pale horse. And the name of him sitting on it was Death, and Hell followed with him. And authority was given to them over the fourth part of the earth, to kill with the sword and with hunger and with death and by the beasts of the earth."

> (Revelation 6:7-8, MKJV)

At this stage, the narrative in Revelation 6 pauses to indicate that the saints, who have been warning populations and governments about transgressions, will subsequently face oppression and persecution. The following verses are examined in the subsequent chapter, which addresses the Last Days. Attention must now be directed to another significant development anticipated to occur around 2030.

Robotic warfare

Battlefields are frequently marked by significant casualties among soldiers. Wars often reach a point of exhaustion due to the high number of fatalities. In many cases, victory is determined by which side retains more soldiers.

Military engineers and commanders have therefore sought methods to save their own soldiers' lives while inflicting losses on the enemy. This pursuit has driven the development of armaments capable of continuing combat operations in situations where human soldiers cannot.

The Bible describes such a quest for supremacy:

"A fire devours before them, and behind them a flame burns. The land is as the garden of Eden before them, and behind them a desolate wilderness. Yes, and nothing shall escape them.

As the appearance of horses is its appearance; and as war horses, so they run.

They shall leap like the noise of chariots on the tops of mountains, like the noise of a flame of fire that devours the stubble, like a strong people set in battle order.

Before their face the people shall be much pained; all faces shall gather blackness.

They shall run like mighty ones. They shall climb the wall like men of war, and they shall march each one on his way, and they shall not break their ranks.

And each one shall not press his brother; they each go in his paths. And if they fall behind their weapons, they shall not be cut off."

(Joel 2:3-8, MKJV)

This is made possible with military drone and robotic technology. More sophisticated machines with Artificial Intelligence will appear towards the end.

Bio and chemical warfare

Governments often recognize the futility of destroying entire cities solely out of animosity toward their inhabitants, especially when these citizens resist or challenge authority. Ultimately, such actions result in ruined cities that become uninhabitable. This raises questions regarding the purpose of these conflicts and whether it is possible to eliminate populations without demolishing urban infrastructure.

Biological and chemical weapons have been developed for such purposes. Additionally, low-yield nuclear weapons, often referred to as "dirty" bombs, can generate magnetic shock waves that incapacitate both civilians and soldiers, preventing further resistance. This approach enables the destruction or incapacitation of populations while preserving urban infrastructure for subsequent occupation by opposing forces.

"And to them it was given that they should not kill them, but that they should be tormented five months. And their torment was like a scorpion's torment when he stings a man.

And in those days men will seek death and will not find it. And they will long to die, and death will flee from them.

And the shapes of the locusts were like horses prepared for battle. And on their heads were as it were crowns like gold, and their faces were like the faces of men."

(Revelation 9:5-7, MKJV)

Such weapons are currently under development, and authoritarian leaders are likely to employ them aggressively to achieve their objectives.

Citizens under these regimes may remain passive, while others suffer severe consequences. The ultimate accountability of these leaders and their populations will be addressed in the following chapter.

Future conflicts are likely to involve the use, study, and refinement of chemical and biological warfare. This development presents significant concerns, as authoritarian leaders may escalate their ruthlessness in response to increasing abuses and atrocities.

The Time of the Gentiles

The decline in global influence and power among English-speaking nations has been interpreted by some scholars as signaling the emergence of the 'time of the Gentiles.' This period is viewed as a resurgence of the image described in the Book of Daniel.

The kingdoms depicted in Daniel's vision exerted successive influence over the Promised Land of Israel from the era of the prophet Daniel to the First Advent of the Messiah. Each kingdom achieved global prominence before ultimately dissolving. Some interpretations suggest that these kingdoms will reemerge in the Last Days, simultaneously gaining strength and presenting a significant threat to the Israelites residing in Jerusalem. The possibility of their concurrent existence raises important questions regarding the fulfillment of prophecy.

> "This image's head was of fine gold; his breast and his arms were of silver; his belly and his thighs were of bronze;
>
> his legs were of iron; his feet were part of iron and part of clay.
>
> You watched until a stone was cut out without hands, which struck the image upon its feet which were of iron and clay, and broke them to pieces."
>
> (Daniel 2:32-34, MKJV)

The entire statue is predicted to collapse. It is possible that these kingdoms will coexist during the Last Days. Historians have identified and acknowledged these kingdoms as follows:

1) The 'head of gold' refers to Nebuchadnezzar, king of Babylon. The region corresponding to ancient Babylon is now primarily within the borders of modern Iraq. Saddam Hussein sought to revive the Babylonian Empire, but his efforts were curtailed by the United States during the Gulf War. With the diminishing influence of the United States and the United Kingdom, questions arise regarding the potential resurgence of Iraq as a regional power. Iraq may again attempt to assert control over Kuwait's substantial oil reserves, potentially positioning itself as a major

energy supplier comparable to Saudi Arabia. Such a development could lead to the emergence of a regional power characterized by a more moderate interpretation of Islam.

2) The chest of the statue in Daniel's prophecy is interpreted as representing Cyrus the Great of Persia, whose empire originated in the region now known as Iran. The two arms symbolize the development of the Medo-Persian Empire. In contemporary times, Iran has become a significant exporter of military equipment and is frequently cited as a supporter of terrorism. Its influence in the Middle East is expanding, posing a considerable threat to Jewish communities in Israel and other regions. Furthermore, Iran is increasingly adopting a more radical form of Islam and is rapidly emerging as a major military power in the Middle East.

3) The 'legs of Iron' referred to the Greco-Macedonian Empire, led by Alexander the Great, which originated in Greece. The predominant religion in this region is now Orthodox Christianity, which stands in opposition to Roman Catholicism. The influence of this ideology is observable in the Baltic states of the European Union and in Russia. Initially, some of these states are expected to become fully integrated into the European Union and may eventually assume leadership roles among the Baltic States of Central Europe. While they are likely to achieve full NATO membership, they are also projected to oppose Western Europe's liberal values. In this context, Orthodox Christianity is expected to challenge Roman Catholicism in the West, particularly given the presence of liberalism, which is considered incompatible with Orthodox Christian doctrine.

4) The 'feet of iron mixed with clay' have been interpreted as representing the Roman Empire, governed by Roman Emperors and centered in the region now known as Italy. The influence and expansion of the Roman Catholic Church are well documented, and its reach is expected to impact Jerusalem. In contemporary terms, this influence may be reflected in the expanding role of the European Union in Western Europe, particularly in Germany and Austria. The increasing membership and expansion of NATO are perceived as potential threats by countries in the Far East, such as Russia and China. Additionally, the Baltic states of Central Europe are likely to form a more right-wing coalition, which may further isolate liberal Western Europe.

The four elements of the statue described by the prophet Daniel are expected to form distinct religious power blocs during the period known as the Last Days.

1) Roman Catholicism
        (Italy, Germany, France, Spain, Austria – Generally Western nations)
2) Orthodox Christianity
        (Greece, Romania, Georgia, Serbia, Russia – Generally Baltic and Eastern states)
3) Shia Islam
        (Iran, Azerbaijan, Bahrain, Lebanon, Bahrain, some Iran)
4) Sunni Islam
        (Turkey, Egypt, historic Iraq, Saudi Arabia, mostly Northern Africa)

These religions have already achieved global dissemination and may be utilized by world governments to influence individuals against the Second Advent and the Messiah.

Protestant Christianity

Protestant Christianity is experiencing a decline, paralleling the diminishing influence of the Church of England. The faith, originally established by settlers who left Europe in protest against Roman Catholicism, is currently waning. These settlers, who departed before the persecution by the Church of Rome in the 1600s, following the Middle Ages, sought to shape new societies in regions such as the United States, Canada, Australia, New Zealand, and South Africa. Over time, they abandoned the observance of the Sabbath and adopted the view that the Ten Commandments were no longer binding, thereby justifying worship on Sunday rather than the traditional Sabbath. This theological stance is often considered inconsistent with scriptural teachings. It is argued that because Protestant groups continue to observe Sunday worship as instituted by the Church of Rome and formalized in the fourth century, they remain susceptible to papal influence.

Protestant Christianity is expected to face criticism from both Roman Catholicism and Islam. Alongside the decline of English-speaking nations, sometimes identified as the Lost Ten Tribes of Israel, Protestant Christianity is projected to diminish further. Eschatological interpretations suggest that, during the period known as the Last Days, adherents will experience oppression and a significant reduction in influence until the anticipated arrival of the Messiah. Consequently, Protestant Christianity is not expected to play a significant role in the final conflict described in these theological frameworks.

Four opposing religions

The two principal Western religions in Europe represent divergent forms of Christianity, both of which are considered apostate to some extent and are expected to oppose the Messiah and adherents of Commandment-Keeping Christianity upon His return. In contrast, the two major Eastern religions encompass distinct branches of Islam, which, according to the Quran, do not recognize Jesus as the Christ and are anticipated to resist the Messiah at His return through military conflict. Following the decline of the United States and the United Kingdom's influence, these four religious groups are projected to rise in prominence and pose significant threats to the people of Israel. In the eschatological period known as the Last Days, these groups are expected to engage in military confrontations. Upon the Messiah's miraculous return, it is asserted that these groups will be defeated, as the general populace will seek the governance and peace offered by the Son of God.

> "Then the iron, the clay, the bronze, the silver, and the gold were broken to pieces together. And they became like the chaff of the summer threshing floors. And the wind carried them away, so that no place was found for them. And the stone that struck the image became a great mountain and filled the whole earth."

(Daniel 2:35, MKJV)

This passage addresses the four blocs of nations, each associated with distinct religions, that will form the coalition opposing the Messiah at His return. According to this interpretation, the Messiah will expose the theological errors of these groups, which are considered flawed, and will resist Christ at His Second Advent.

"And in the days of these kings, the **God of Heaven shall set up** a kingdom which shall never be destroyed. And the kingdom shall not be left to other peoples, but it shall crush and destroy all these kingdoms, and it shall stand forever.

Because you saw that the stone was cut out of the mountain **without hands**, and that it crushes the iron, the bronze, the clay, the silver, and the gold, the great God has made known to the king what shall occur after this. And the dream is certain, and its meaning is sure"

(Daniel 2:44-45, MKJV)[Emphasis mine]

The return of the Messiah is anticipated to fundamentally transform religious paradigms. It is expected that the extent to which these four religious groups have diverged from authentic worship will become evident. Subsequently, warfare is projected to cease, and governments will no longer be able to exploit religion as a justification for conflict. This period is characterized by the establishment of global peace. The legitimacy of the supernatural Second Advent and the authority of the Son of God are presented as incontrovertible.

Summary

The narrative of the Prophet Jonah reveals several recurring sequences that remain relevant.

Nineveh, a gentile city, was granted **40** days to repent, and did so successfully. This outcome suggests a favorable precedent for gentile nations at the time of the Messiah's return.

The disciples of Jesus Christ were given **40** days to address any unbelief prior to Pentecost, enabling them to receive the gifts of the Spirit of God, including healing and speaking in other languages. They fulfilled this requirement.

The Jewish population in Jerusalem was allotted **40** years to repent from the legal modifications and replacement laws instituted by the Pharisees and Sadducees, which were seen as contrary to God's Law. Their failure to do so resulted in the destruction of Jerusalem and the Old Testament Temple.

The lost House of Israel, comprising the Ten Tribes of the northern kingdom who were dispersed and eventually migrated to what are termed the 'free worlds,' have been allotted **40** Jubilees to repent and restore authentic worship of the Creator God by faithfully following the Ministry of the Messiah. While many evangelists and pastors are dedicated to this mission, opposition from liberal governments and associated advocacy groups is perceived as suppressing traditional Christianity. As a result, it is anticipated that the 'free worlds' will experience a decline in power, wealth, and influence.

Interpretations of the prophecies of Jonah, other prophets, and the teachings of Jesus Christ indicate that the year 2030 will hold particular significance. Forty Jubilees after the crucifixion of Jesus Christ, regarded as a profound injustice, the period allotted for repentance by the Lost Ten Tribes of Israel residing in the 'free worlds' will conclude. The prohibition of displaying the Ten Commandments in courtrooms is seen as evidence of societal disregard for foundational principles. The exclusion of Christian education from schools is viewed as detrimental to the moral development of children. The discontinuation of daily prayer in parliamentary settings is believed to undermine Christian values in governmental decision-making. Permitting large corporations to ignore scriptural guidance, resulting in environmental pollution and resource exploitation, is expected to precipitate unforeseen disasters. Similarly, neglecting established agricultural principles is likely to cause soil degradation and insufficient healthy food supplies. The absence of prayerful consideration in major decisions is anticipated to result in significant errors.

Following 2030, it is anticipated that gentile nations will rise in prominence. Authoritarian leaders are expected to prevail, creating hardships for the descendants of the Lost Ten Tribes of Israel. The 'free worlds' are projected to experience decline and adversity. Support for the Jewish population in the Promised Land may also diminish. The question of who will ultimately deliver Jerusalem remains unresolved. The onset of the Last Days is expected to coincide with the reduction and eventual elimination of global influence by English-speaking nations.

Christians who observe the Sabbath, the seventh day of the week, are also aware of the anticipated millennial reign of the Messiah, the Lord Jesus Christ.

This narrative is expected to culminate positively, with a period of glory following the Messiah's return. In the interim, English-speaking Western populations, identified as the Lost Ten Tribes of Israel, are predicted to lose influence and power. Atheistic nations and those adhering to other religions are expected to rise, particularly after 2030. The descendants of the twelve tribes of Israel will undergo significant trials, as it is believed that God seeks to determine who will repent and return to Him.

It is hoped that this book has imparted wisdom to its readers. The era of the gentiles has arrived, and the approach of the Last Days is imminent.

The Last Days

After 2030, the period referred to as the final Last Days will commence, marking the completion of 40 Jubilees since the Crucifixion.

Governments that once appeared Christian have prohibited Bible reading in official settings, banned prayer in parliaments, and removed Christian education from schools. The Creator's purpose of expanding His Family on earth now faces significant challenges. We cannot seek deliverance from God while simultaneously behaving as though He does not exist.

The Bible outlines periods of severe hardship for humanity. Although these events may seem implausible, they remain within the realm of possibility. We will continue our discussion from the previous chapter.

Since the emergence of the Four Horsemen, a pause is evident in the scriptural narrative. Evangelists have issued warnings to individuals, communities, and governments.

In response, certain governments have persecuted these evangelists.

> "And when He had opened the fifth seal, I saw under the altar the souls of those who had been slain for the Word of God, and for the testimony which they held.
>
> And they cried with a loud voice, saying, Until when, Master, holy and true, do You not judge and avenge our blood on those who dwell on the earth?
>
> And white robes were given to each one of them. And it was said to them that they should rest yet for a little time, until both their fellow servants and their brothers (those about to be killed as they were) should have their number made complete."
>
> (Revelation 6:9-11, MKJV)

The elimination and global prohibition of Christian pastors and evangelists from preaching, particularly after 2030, is interpreted as a sign of the arrival of the Last Days. At this point, it is anticipated that the Earth will appear to have turned against humanity.

> "And when He had opened the sixth seal, I looked, and behold, there was a great earthquake. And the sun became black as sackcloth of hair, and the moon became like blood."
>
> (Revelation 6:12, MKJV)

Humankind made several mistakes that will lead to earthquakes:

According to the biblical account in Genesis, the construction of the first high-rise building complex, the Tower of Babel, was halted when God caused the people to speak different languages. This intervention disrupted their collaboration and led to their dispersal. In contemporary times, however, nations have resumed the construction of tall buildings, which may contribute to localized pressure on the earth's crust. The narrative suggests that human settlement should ideally be distributed across agricultural communities and small towns.

> "Woe to those who join house to house,
> laying field to field, until the end of space,
> and you are made to dwell alone in the
> middle of the land!"

(Isaiah 5:8, MKJV)

Secondly, many nations have pumped out large volumes of oil, leaving huge holes in the earth's crust.

Thirdly, instead of forming towns around rivers, many nations are pumping a tremendous amount of water from underground, emptying huge underground lakes and rivers, creating vast sections of empty space in the earth's crust.

Fourthly, global warming is building pressure in dormant volcanoes, and many will eventually erupt, releasing lava at points in the Earth's crust.

A major earthquake is predicted to occur, triggering additional volcanic eruptions. The resulting dust could encircle the Earth, obscuring the sun and moon. Such atmospheric effects may lead to global crop failures, similar to the aftermath of the 535 AD Krakatoa eruption in Indonesia, when volcanic ash remained in the atmosphere for over a year. According to some interpretations, these events are seen as consequences of human actions, with warnings found in scriptural texts. Numerous Biblical passages address principles of safe living.

The remainder of Revelation 6 details the consequences following the major earthquake. Revelation 7 then records the completion of the final enumeration of God's servants.

Revelation 8 presents a scenario involving a meteor impacting the earth. A comparable event occurred on Jupiter in recent years, as documented by the Hubble telescope.

A meteor consists of frozen rock, sand, and gases. Upon entering the solar system, solar radiation causes the frozen gases to evaporate, which are then dispersed by the solar wind. The gravitational pull of a large planet can separate the rock and sand, resulting in individual fragments striking the planet at various locations as it rotates.

Notice the exact prophetic description, which could well be accurate.

"The first angel sounded, and there followed hail and fire mixed with blood, and they were cast on the earth. And the third part of trees was burned up, and all green grass was burned up.

And the second angel sounded, and as it were a great mountain burning with fire was cast into the sea. And the third part of the sea became blood.

And the third part of the creatures in the sea, those having souls, died; and the third part of the ships was destroyed.

And the third angel sounded, and a great star burning like a lamp fell from the heaven, and it fell on the third part of the rivers and on the fountains of waters.

And the name of the star is called Wormwood, and a third part of the waters became wormwood. And many men died from the waters, because they were made bitter.

And the fourth angel sounded, and the third part of the sun was stricken, and the third part of the moon, and the third part of the stars, so that the third part of them was darkened, and the day did not appear for a third part of it, and the night also."

(Revelation 8:7-12, MKJV)

Following such a global calamity, it is reasonable to expect that individuals and governments might turn to the Bible, previously neglected, in search of explanations for these catastrophic events. However, it remains uncertain whether a divided global population can collectively seek guidance from scripture and support one another.

The rest of the book of Revelation will be explained in another book on the Apocalypse. See the link below:

Apocalypse: Revealing Revelation

https://www.amazon.com/gp/product/B0B7HP9Y6G?ref_=dbs_m_mng_rwt_calw_tkin_21&storeType=ebooks

Natural disasters may compel humanity to either seek reconciliation with God or engage in conflict with one another during the final wars. The return of the Messiah is anticipated when humanity demonstrates readiness to receive Him and turn to the Creator.

In reference to both the period preceding the destruction of Jerusalem and the potential self-destruction of humanity, Christ offered the following observations regarding the human condition:

"for then shall be great tribulation, such as has not been since the beginning of the world to this time; no, nor ever shall be.

And unless those days should be shortened, no flesh would be saved. But for the elect's sake, those days shall be shortened."

(Matthew 24:21-22, MKJV)

Like wayward children, we will be repentant and understand that our Heavenly Father was right after all.

Appendix A

At the outset of His ministry, Jesus Christ, the Messiah, made a significant observation. However, contemporary readers often overlook its importance and fail to grasp its full significance.

"And He came to Nazareth, where He had been brought up. And, as His custom was, He went in to the synagogue on the Sabbath day and stood up to read. And the book of the prophet Isaiah was handed to Him. And unrolling the book, He found the place where it was written,

"The Spirit of the Lord is on Me; because of this He has anointed Me to proclaim the Gospel to the poor. He has sent me to heal the brokenhearted, to proclaim deliverance to the captives, and new sight to the blind, to set at liberty those having been crushed, to proclaim the acceptable year of the Lord."

And rolling up the book, returning it to the attendant, He sat down. And the eyes of all in the synagogue were fastened on Him. And He began to say to them, Today this Scripture is fulfilled in your ears.

And all bore witness to Him and wondered at the gracious words which came out of His mouth. And they said, Is this not Joseph's son?"

(Luke 4:16-22, MKJV)

Why were these words so gracious?

If the Jewish population had demonstrated repentance and readiness for divine rule, Jesus Christ intended to implement the Kingdom of God as a central aspect of his mission. He aimed to establish the Jubilee year in 31 AD, as prescribed by Mosaic Law. This mandate, however, had been neglected by the Pharisees, Sadducees, and the Levitical priesthood of the period. Furthermore, Roman authorities and the Herod family, an Arab political elite who gained power in Jerusalem through Roman support, actively obstructed the establishment of the Jubilee.

Jesus is described as a descendant of King David and was prophesied to become the King of Jerusalem and Israel. The three wise men from the East, who were familiar with the scriptures, visited him and presented gifts. Herod attempted to kill Jesus, and other influential families also sought to eliminate him. These actions were intended to prevent the implementation of the Jubilee system, which was designed to provide relief from persistent poverty.

A comprehensive explanation of the biblical Jubilee system is necessary to clarify its potential role in preventing social and economic conflict.

The Jubilee System

As civilization advances and economic activity expands, disparities in success among individuals and families are inevitable. Some farmers benefit from favorable weather, while others face drought. Some individuals may work diligently, yet health challenges can hinder their productivity. Unpredictable events, such as a cloudburst destroying crops or lightning striking a farmer's shed, can cause significant setbacks. These calamities may force families to sell essential tools, machinery, or even farmland to afford basic necessities. In some cases, families become trapped in a cycle of poverty, compelled to work as laborers to survive. If this cycle persists, future generations may endure exploitation by landlords and mistreatment. Historically, such conditions have led to collective action by the impoverished against the wealthy and corrupt authorities, resulting in conflict and revolution. The French Revolution serves as a historical example of these dynamics.

It is evident from theological perspectives that God does not desire people to live in servitude or for wars to occur.

Conversely, a communist system may suppress innovation, as individuals may become resigned to an oppressive government. In such environments, entrepreneurs may withhold ideas that could benefit society. It is essential for individuals to have opportunities to reap the rewards of their hard work and innovation; otherwise, motivation to improve and advance society diminishes.

Accordingly, the Jubilee system given to Israel provides a framework that supports both economic innovation and a periodic reset. This mechanism is intended to liberate future generations from the consequences of misfortune and errors made by their predecessors. Isaiah's prophecies regarding the Messiah's first advent highlight Israel's potential to serve as an exemplary society by adhering to God's Law. Ideally, Israel would have become a nation of priests and leaders for the surrounding nations. This vision was partially realized during the reign of King David and, to some extent, under King Solomon. However, Solomon's alliances and acceptance of foreign practices led to apostasy, resulting in Israel's eventual captivity. Nevertheless, Isaiah foretold a future in which a true Leader would arise in Jerusalem, ushering in a period of greater prosperity and justice.

> "Your people also will all be righteous; they will inherit the land forever, the branch of My planting, the work of My hands, so that I may be glorified.
>
> A little one will become a thousand, and a small one a strong nation: I Jehovah will hasten it in its time."
>
> (Isaiah 60:21-22, MKJV)

The implementation of the Law of God, including the Jubilee economic model, is anticipated to commence with the arrival of the Messiah.

> "The Spirit of the Lord Jehovah is on Me; because Jehovah has anointed Me to preach the Gospel to the poor; He has sent Me to

bind up the broken-hearted, to proclaim liberty to the captives, and the opening of the prison to those who are bound;

to preach the **acceptable year of Jehovah** and the day of vengeance of our God; to comfort all who mourn;

to appoint to those who mourn in Zion, to give to them beauty for ashes, the oil of joy for mourning, the mantle of praise for the spirit of heaviness; so that they might be called trees of righteousness, the planting of Jehovah, that He might be glorified.

And they will build the old wastes, they will raise up the ruins of former times. And they will repair the waste cities, the ruins of many generations."

(Isaiah 61:1-4, MKJV) [Emphasis mine]

Jesus proclaimed the coming of the Jubilee economic reset, and those who heard Him were eager to receive this message of hope. The prospect of implementing the Jubilee system promised improved conditions for the poor and marginalized. However, the Jewish people were unprepared, as they remained bound by sin and corruption. Their lack of righteousness necessitated that Jesus demonstrate humanity's collective shortcomings through the crucifixion of the innocent Son of God. As a result, nations have faced significant consequences. The occurrence of world wars was foretold, attributed to the widespread abandonment of God and His Law.

Functioning of the Jubilee System

How would the Jubilee system function in practice? The following section will examine its specific mechanisms.

.

"You shall sow your field six years, and you shall prune your vineyard six years, and gather in the fruit of it.

But in the seventh year shall be a sabbath of rest to the land, a sabbath for Jehovah. You shall neither sow your field, nor prune your vineyard.

You shall not reap that which grows of its own accord of your harvest, neither gather the grapes of your undressed vine. It is a year of rest to the land.

And the sabbath of the land shall be food for you, for you and for your servant, and for your slave woman and for your hired servant, and for your stranger who stays with you,

and for your cattle, and for the beast that is in your land, shall all the increase of it be for food."

(Leviticus 25:3-7, MKJV)

Every seventh year, the land should remain unploughed. Trees and seeds planted in previous years will continue to grow, providing food, although potentially in reduced quantities. However, if the land has been properly prepared during the preceding six years, food supplies should remain sufficient. This period allows the soil to remain undisturbed, enabling roots to develop and subterranean organisms, such as worms, to create tunnels and thrive. Increased soil cavities enhance water absorption during rainfall. As a result, the soil is rejuvenated, often leading to a significantly improved harvest in the following year.

In various countries, farmers have implemented rotational systems in which one-seventh of their farmland is left fallow each year. While this approach offers some benefits, fully observing the Sabbath year is intended to maximize the recovery of soil, plants, and animal populations.

"And you shall number seven sabbaths of years to you, seven times seven years. And the time of the seven sabbaths of years shall be forty-nine years to you.

Then you shall cause the trumpet of the jubilee to sound on the tenth of the seventh month; in the day of atonement, the trumpet shall sound throughout all your land.

And you shall make the fiftieth year holy, one year, and proclaim liberty throughout the land to all its inhabitants. It shall be a jubilee to you, and you shall return each man to his possession, and you shall return each man to his family.

That fiftieth year shall be a jubilee to you. You shall not sow, neither reap that which grows of itself in it, nor gather in it of your undressed vine.

For it is the jubilee. It shall be holy to you. You shall eat the increase of it out of the field.

In the year of this jubilee you shall return each man to his possession.

(Leviticus 25:8-13, MKJV)

In the fiftieth year, families can reclaim land that previous generations were compelled to sell to survive. This process enables families to break the cycle of poverty. The Jubilee offers hope to those experiencing hardship, promising future liberation from oppressive conditions.

The accumulation of wealth by the affluent will be curtailed, preventing unchecked property speculation and the destruction of others' livelihoods. The wealthy will remain aware that workers will eventually reclaim the land they currently cultivate. This process constitutes an economic reset.

Urban expansion into densely populated areas will be limited, thereby reducing concentrated heat generation and mitigating adverse weather patterns such as increased wind speeds. Additionally, preventing excessive development in specific locations will reduce pressure on the earth's crust, decreasing the likelihood of heightened earthquake activity that could damage or render buildings uninhabitable.

The concentration of wealth among elites will be limited, reducing their ability to influence government decisions through lobbying that exacerbates poverty. As a result, the incidence of civil disturbances and crime is expected to decline, and the risk of civil war may be mitigated.

A critical consideration is how affluent individuals and their economies will adapt to the disruption caused by the economic reset. However, since the timing of the reset is predetermined, stakeholders can anticipate its occurrence and incorporate it into their decisions, contracts, and business arrangements.

"According to the number of years after the jubilee you shall buy of your neighbor, according to the number of years of the fruits he shall sell to you.

According to the number of years you shall increase the price of it, and according to the fewness of years you shall diminish the price of it, for he is selling to you the number of crops."

(Leviticus 25:15-16, MKJV)

Contemporary economies are unlikely to implement such a transformation without significant challenges. A sudden economic reset by governments would likely lead to widespread disruption, potentially triggering civil unrest and even conflict. Effective implementation would require a formal declaration and an extended period of preparation, potentially spanning several decades and incorporating measures such as land Sabbaths. The establishment of a just and effective government is essential to address potential misuse of the Jubilee economic model and to ensure a stable transition.

"And you shall not oppress one another. But you shall fear your God. For I am Jehovah your God.

And you shall do My statutes, and keep My judgments and do them. And you shall dwell in the land in safety.

And the land shall yield its fruits, and you shall eat your fill and dwell in it in safety.

And if you shall say, What shall we eat the seventh year? Behold, we shall not sow nor gather in our increase!

Then I will command My blessing on you in the sixth year, and it shall bring forth fruit for three years.

And you shall sow the eighth year, and eat of old fruit until the ninth year; until its fruits come in, you shall eat the old fruit.

The land shall not be sold forever; for the land is Mine. For you are strangers and pilgrims with Me.

And in all the land of your possession you shall grant a redemption for the land.

(Leviticus 25:17-24, MKJV)

However, land cannot be sold and resold indefinitely to the extent that the original family is unable to identify and reclaim their ancestral property in the fiftieth year. The land must remain accessible to the original family, who may redeem it with payment even before the Jubilee year if circumstances permit.

"If your brother has become poor, and has sold his property, and if any of his relatives comes to redeem it, then he shall redeem that which his brother sold.

And if the man has no redeemer, and he himself is able to redeem it, and he has enough for its redemption;

then let him count the years of the sale of it, and restore the overplus to the man to whom he sold it, so that he may return to his possession.

But if he is not able to restore to him, then that which is sold shall remain in the hand of him that has bought it until the year of jubilee. And in the jubilee it shall go out, and he shall return to his possession."

(Leviticus 25:25-28, MKJV)

However, houses located in city centres are not returned during the Jubilee year. These properties may remain permanently with the individuals who have acquired them through their own efforts and payment. Provided the family can maintain the property, ownership can be retained indefinitely.

"And if a man sells a dwelling house in a walled city, then he may redeem it within a whole year after it is sold. He may redeem it within a full year.

> And if it is not redeemed within the time of a full year, then the house in the walled city shall be made sure forever to its buyer throughout his generations. It shall not go out in the jubilee."

(Leviticus 25:29-30, MKJV)

However, houses situated on small plots and smallholdings adhere to the Jubilee system. These properties are returned to families in the fiftieth year.

> "But the houses of the villages which have no walls around them shall be counted as the field of the country. They may be redeemed, and they shall go out in the jubilee."

(Leviticus 25:31, MKJV)

Urban houses owned by government officials remained the permanent property of their families. During the Old Testament period, the Levites served as both priests and government authorities. With the subsequent establishment of the monarchy, royal officials likely resided in major cities, and their urban residences also remained within their families, exempt from transfer during the Jubilee year. If such a house were sold to a non-governmental family, it would revert to the official's family during the Jubilee.

> "As to the cities of the Levites, the houses of the cities of their possession, the Levites shall have a never-ending redemption.

And if a man purchases a house from the Levites, then the house that was sold and the city of his possession shall go out in the year of jubilee. For the houses of the cities of the Levites are their possession among the sons of Israel.

But the field of the open land of their cities may not be sold, for it is theirs forever."

(Leviticus 25:32-35, MKJV)

In the remainder of this chapter in the Bible, it is stated that owners and landlords are expected to treat servants and workers with mercy and to show respect for all individuals, as all are considered God's creation. During the Jubilee, servants may recover lost land and houses within smallholdings, and any previous acts of harshness may have consequences for the perpetrators. If these consequences do not occur during their lifetime, they are believed to manifest on Judgment Day, specifically at the White Throne Judgment of God following the second resurrection, as described in Revelation.

Therefore, according to these principles, no family should be rendered homeless. Additionally, another law of God is introduced:

"And when you reap the harvest of your land, you shall not wholly reap the corner of your field. And you shall not gather the gleaning of your harvest.

And you shall not glean your vineyard. And you shall not gather the leavings of your vineyard. You shall leave them for the poor and the stranger. I am Jehovah your God."

(Leviticus 19:9-10, MKJV)

Farmers are required to leave the corners and edges of their harvest, as well as any excess food, for those in need. This practice ensures that provisions remain available for the poor. Jesus affirmed this principle during his travels with his disciples.

"At that time Jesus went through the grain fields on the sabbath day. And His disciples were hungry, and began to pluck the heads of grain and to eat.

But when the Pharisees saw, they said to Him, Behold, your disciples do that which it is not lawful to do on the sabbath day."

(Matthew 21:1-2, MKJV)

Jesus and His disciples did not commit theft from the farmer, as the law granted His disciples the right to harvest the corners of the field. Additionally, the law ensured that no one needed to go hungry, even on the Sabbath.

If nations adhered to God's law, homelessness and hunger could be prevented. However, corrupt so-called "Christian" governments have permitted the wealthy to oppress the poor, resulting in widespread homelessness and hunger. Consequently, God may forsake these former "Christian" nations and permit atheistic ideologies to prevail in the coming years. As a result, societies may abandon democracy and other freedoms, potentially allowing communism to take hold and leading to the loss of religious liberty.

"Her rulers in her midst are like wolves tearing the prey, to shed blood and to destroy souls, to get unjust gain.

And her prophets have daubed themselves with lime, seeing vanity and divining lies to them, saying, So says the Lord Jehovah; when Jehovah has not spoken.

The people of the land have used oppression and practiced robbery, and they have troubled the poor and needy. Yea, they have oppressed the stranger without right.

And I sought for a man among them who should wall up a wall for the land, and stand in the break before me, that I should not destroy it. But I did not find one."

(Ezekiel 22:27-30, MKJV)

The Jubilee economic model is designed to prevent families from remaining trapped in cycles of poverty. It also aims to limit the accumulation of excessive wealth by certain families, thereby reducing their ability to influence governments or incite conflict. By addressing these economic disparities, the model seeks to prevent both civil and international wars. Proponents argue that its implementation could have averted major conflicts such as World War I and World War II, and may help to prevent a future global conflict.

According to Christian tradition, Jesus proclaimed the restoration of the Jubilee system at the beginning of his ministry in 27 AD.

"And He came to Nazareth, where He had
been brought up. And, as His custom was,
He went in to the synagogue on the Sabbath
day and stood up to read.
 And the book of the prophet Isaiah was
handed to Him. And unrolling the book, He
found the place where it was written,
"The Spirit of the Lord is on Me; because of
this He has anointed Me to proclaim the
Gospel to the poor. He has sent me to heal
the brokenhearted, to proclaim deliverance
to the captives, and new sight to the blind, to
set at liberty those having been crushed,
to proclaim the acceptable year of the Lord."
And rolling up the book, returning it to the
attendant, He sat down. And the eyes of all
in the synagogue were fastened on Him.
And He began to say to them, Today this
Scripture is fulfilled in your ears."
(Luke 4:16-21, MKJV)

Although Jesus might have formally reinstated it in 30
or 31 AD, His execution by the ruling elite prevented this.
Calculating forty Jubilee cycles from that time leads to
the year 2030, which some interpret as a critical moment
for formerly Christian nations to engage in self-
examination and repentance for corruption and
oppression. Without such reflection and change, it is
argued that the rise of atheistic regimes will make global
reform unattainable until the anticipated return of the
Messiah. This raises the question of whether these nations
will choose to repent.

Christian eschatological interpretations hold that Jesus
was crucified in 30 to 31 AD, after which Israel and

Jerusalem were given forty years to repent before facing destruction by non-believers. By analogy, it is suggested that formerly Christian nations have forty Jubilee cycles to repent and observe the Commandments, including the Sabbath. After 2030, it is anticipated that secular regimes may dominate, leading to increased oppression and persecution of Christians, as well as efforts to re-educate populations and suppress biblical teachings. According to this perspective, when these regimes ultimately engage in conflict to advance their ideologies and humanity faces existential threats, the Messiah is expected to return to Jerusalem, as described in the Book of Revelation.

Appendix B

Invasion of the British Isles

Over a millennium ago, Islamic forces invaded Spain from North Africa. The geographical proximity of these regions facilitated the conquest across the sea. The campaign began in 711 CE and culminated in the establishment of a caliphate from 929 to 1031. During this period, Muslims governed Christians and Jews while permitting the practice of their respective faiths. Concurrently, Muslims also maintained control over Jerusalem.

Numerous sources provide evidence of this historical period. One such source is provided below:

https://www.bbc.co.uk/religion/religions/islam/history/spain_1.shtml

Following this period, oppression intensified. Christians and Jews faced higher taxation than Muslims and were relegated to subordinate social status. Concurrently, Islamic forces advanced toward Rome from both Spain and Jerusalem, which alarmed the Roman Catholic priesthood due to perceived threats from both the East and the West. In response, Christian crusades were organized from Rome. The First Crusade advanced eastward and recaptured Jerusalem in 1099, removing the city from Islamic control. Additional crusades aimed to reclaim Spain, Portugal, and the Baltic states in Central Europe. These efforts were framed as the liberation of Europe in the name of Christianity, leading to the restoration of Papal authority and a period of Islamic retreat. However, the enforcement of Roman Catholicism contributed to the spread of the so-called Dark Middle Ages across Europe, including the British Isles, until the Reformation initiated by Martin Luther in the 16th century.

The monarchies of Europe clashed during World War I, a conflict that was not fully resolved and was further disrupted by the outbreak of the Spanish flu. Persistent unresolved issues and the subsequent oppression of Germany contributed to the outbreak of World War II. Following the United States' victory and its demonstration of power through the use of nuclear weapons, a new global threat emerged from the Far East, particularly in the form of Communism and Socialism.

The problem with Capitalism

Capitalism emerged as a dominant force in the West, including Britain. Although the Westminster model of democracy was regarded as a solution and other nations were encouraged to adopt democratic systems, a significant flaw persisted. According to biblical precedent, God anticipated such challenges for Israel millennia ago and instituted the Jubilee system. This system ensured that families retained the benefits of their labor and that inheritance was preserved across generations. In the face of unforeseen hardships such as drought, conflict, or governmental corruption, the family farm functioned as a crucial safety net. Every seven years, families could repurchase land sold due to hardship, and every fifty years, during the Jubilee year, they could reclaim family land without cost. This approach was designed to prevent the entrenchment of class systems and to guarantee families access to land for subsistence agriculture. While urban homes were excluded from the Jubilee system, rural family farms and homes were intended to be restored to their original owners.

Western democracies did not adopt the Jubilee system, and even within Israel, elites resisted its implementation. This resistance contributed to significant socioeconomic challenges in Europe and the broader Western world. Over time, land ownership became prohibitively expensive, effectively excluding many families from owning family farms. The absence of this safety net particularly affected younger generations, who faced rising living costs and limited access to affordable housing. Unlike previous generations who could rely on family resources for support, young people encountered barriers to marriage and family formation. Urban living and land ownership became increasingly unaffordable. Additionally, efforts to reduce dependence on fossil fuels, combined with rising energy prices, further diminished the attainability of the lifestyles of previous generations. Consequently, these factors have contributed to stagnant or declining population growth, illustrating the consequences of Western capitalism in the absence of a system akin to the Jubilee.

A major challenge for Western governments is that the sustainability of social welfare programs depends on a continually expanding tax base.

As a result, Western governments increasingly seek additional sources of affordable labor to maintain tax revenues.

Open Borders

Therefore, it is proposed that borders be opened, allowing millions of migrants into Western countries to serve as inexpensive labor and contribute taxes to social security programs. This approach aligns with the European Union's current strategy and, according to some interpretations, was foretold in prophecy.

The Book of Daniel contains a prophecy, believed by some to be divinely inspired, concerning the Last Days leading up to future global conflicts.

> "And as the toes of the feet were part of iron and part of clay, so the kingdom shall be partly strong and partly brittle. And as you saw iron mixed with miry clay, they shall mix themselves with the seed of men. But they shall not cling to one another, even as iron is not mixed with clay."
> (Daniel 2:42-43, MKJV)

However, a significant issue arises.

Northern Africa is predominantly Muslim and faces significant economic challenges. Similar conditions exist in many Middle Eastern countries. Following the United States' war on terror in the Middle East, numerous Muslim-majority nations in the region have experienced economic collapse. As a result, a large proportion of migrants are both Muslim and economically disadvantaged. The question then arises: by what means will these individuals reach Western countries? This situation has facilitated the rise of human trafficking.

According to prophecy given to the Apostle John, the global trade system will collapse in the Last Days, and one of the associated evils will be the trafficking of humans.

> "And the merchants of the earth will weep and mourn over her, for no one buys their cargo any more;
> the cargo of gold, and silver, and precious stones, and of pearls, and fine linen, and purple, and silk, and scarlet, and all thyine wood, and every ivory vessel, and every vessel of very precious wood, and of bronze, and of iron, and of marble,
> and cinnamon, and incenses, and ointment, and frankincense, and wine, and oil, and fine flour and wheat, and beasts, and sheep, and horses, and chariots, **and slaves, and souls of men**."
> (Revelation 18:11-13, MKJV)[Emphasis mine]

Upon arrival in Western nations, many Muslim migrants encounter significant economic disparities and experience culture shock. Their perceptions are shaped by memories of Western military interventions in Muslim-majority countries and by observations of Western lifestyles, which they may view as morally permissive. Some migrants may also perceive a lack of legal and moral values in secularized forms of Christianity. The impact of previous conflicts, such as the wars on terror, can foster resentment and resistance to adopting Western values. Additionally, financial obligations to support families in their countries of origin, often involving payments to human trafficking networks, create further pressures. These factors can contribute to increases in internal crime and, in some cases, local terrorism. The widespread use of technologies such as mobile phones, social media, and encrypted communication platforms facilitates the organization and coordination of criminal activities. Consequently, assimilation into Christian-majority societies is unlikely for many migrants, and the continued presence and growth of the Muslim faith within the European Union may have significant social and cultural implications.

Invasion of Britain

Similar to the historical incursion of Spain and Portugal by Muslim forces from North Africa approximately a millennium ago, a comparable movement is currently occurring, with Britain now serving as the primary focal point.

The ongoing decline of the British Empire since the Second World War has been exacerbated by the demand for inexpensive labor and additional taxpayers. Several English towns, including London, now have Muslim mayors. It is argued that these officials may support increased immigration to expand their voter base and consolidate political influence. Furthermore, it is suggested that such dynamics could influence political decisions both domestically and in international forums such as the United Nations, particularly regarding policies related to Israel. These developments are interpreted by some as significant within the context of eschatological narratives.

Historical accounts indicate that the former northern kingdom of Israel experienced captivity and subsequent migration northward and westward, with successive Roman Empires contributing to further displacement into the British Isles. According to biblical tradition, the descendants of Jacob, known as Israel, were promised dominion over the gates of their enemies, as reflected in the promises made to Abraham.

> "and said, I have sworn by Myself, says Jehovah; because you have done this thing, and have not withheld your son, your only one;
> that in blessing I will bless you, and in multiplying I will multiply your seed like the stars of the heavens, and as the sand which is upon the seashore. And your Seed shall possess the **gate of His enemies**."
> (Genesis 22:16-17, MKJV) [Emphasis mine]

This original covenant was transferred to Isaac:

> "But I will establish My covenant with Isaac, whom Sarah shall bear to you at this set time in the next year."
> (Genesis 17:21, MKJV)

Promises were also made to Ismael, who later became the progenitor of a large family and, eventually, many nations. These descendants are commonly known as

Arabs, who later adopted the Muslim faith. However, the primary focus remained with Isaac.

> "And as for Ishmael, I have heard you.
> Behold, I have blessed him, and will
> make him fruitful, and will multiply him
> exceedingly. He shall father twelve chiefs,
> and I will make him a great nation.
> But I will establish My covenant with
> Isaac, whom Sarah shall bear to you at
> this set time in the next year."
> (Genesis 17:20-21, MKJV)

The grouping of the Arabs as twelve nations in the East aligns with earlier promises. However, these promises were initially designated for Isaac.

Ultimately, the covenant was transferred to Jacob when Esau relinquished it in exchange for food after returning from a hunt, hungry and thirsty.

> "And Jacob said, Swear to me this day.
> And he swore to him, and he sold his
> birthright to Jacob.
> Then Jacob gave Esau bread and soup of
> lentils. And he ate and drank, and rose
> up and went his way. And Esau despised
> his birthright."
> (Genesis 25:33, MKJV)

Ultimately, Esau expressed regret for his decision. Following additional deception involving Isaac, which resulted in the final blessing being bestowed upon Jacob, Esau also sought a blessing and received one.

> "And Esau said to his father, Have you
> but one blessing, my father? Bless me,
> me also, my father. And Esau lifted up
> his voice and wept.
> And Isaac his father answered and said
> to him, Behold! Your dwelling shall be of
> the fatness of the earth and of the dew of
> heaven from above.
> And by your sword you shall live, and
> shall serve your brother. And it shall be
> when you shall have the dominion, you
> shall break his yoke from off your neck."
> (Genesis 27:38-40, MKJV)

A time is anticipated when the Arab nations will overcome this oppression, as will be discussed in the following analysis:

Regarding the covenant that grants Israel control over the gates of its enemies, several historical developments are notable. The Northern Kingdom of Israel was taken captive, and its people migrated northward and then eastward into regions adjacent to the Greek Empire, which later became part of the Roman Empire. Continued oppression contributed to the Israelites' loss of identity, as they generally ceased observing the Sabbath of the Lord. Nevertheless, they did not fully assimilate into these nations and continued to migrate further north and west. The promises given to Isaac in a vision are particularly significant in this context:

> "And Jacob went out from Beer-sheba,
> and went toward Haran.

And he came on a certain place, and stayed there all night, because the sun had set. And he took of the stones of that place, and placed them at his head. And he lay down in that place to sleep.
And he dreamed. And behold! A ladder was set up on the earth, and the top of it reached to Heaven! And behold! The angels of God were ascending and descending on it!
And behold! Jehovah stood above it, and said, I am Jehovah, the God of Abraham your father, and the God of Isaac! The land on which you lie I will give to you and to your seed.
And your seed shall be like the dust of the earth, and you shall **spread abroad to the west, and to the east, and to the north, and to the south. And in you and in your Seed shall all the families of the earth be blessed.** And, behold, I am with you, and will keep you in every place where you go, and will **bring you again into this land**. For I will not leave you until I have done that which I have spoken of to you."
(Genesis 28:10-15, MKJV)[Emphasis mine]

According to this perspective, the descendants of Israel are believed to have spread globally, initially to the northwest toward Britain. Subsequently, English populations migrated westward to America, southward to South Africa, and eastward to Australia and New Zealand.

These groups are described as having been granted prosperity and influence, accompanied by significant responsibilities. The maintenance of Christian values and religious practices is emphasized as essential. However, it is argued that these populations have recently neglected their religious foundations, leading to a loss of protection. This neglect is expected to lead to internal unrest, terrorism, and conflicts that deplete resources and intensify economic pressures. The imposition of restrictive laws by indigenous groups, purportedly under the influence of a revived Roman Empire associated with the European Union, is expected to further reduce their numbers. Questions arise about whether these populations will resist external threats and oppressive measures or become subjugated in foreign nations. Ultimately, it is suggested that their numbers will diminish in the so-called Last Days, until a remnant returns to the Promised Land, as described in prophetic visions.

This narrative asserts that societal decline will originate in Britain, the initial center of these populations. It is claimed that English citizens will experience alienation within their own country and will be susceptible to accepting significant immigration from Arab and other groups. The text predicts that the Muslim faith will become increasingly prominent. Political leaders are described as relinquishing national interests, drawing a parallel to the biblical story of Esau and Jacob, suggesting that Esau will regain inheritance over Jacob due to the latter's abandonment of their religious heritage in the Last Days.

The text claims that an increasing number of appointed mayors in British towns are Muslim, and suggests that this trend will facilitate further immigration and the allocation of public funds to support these communities. It is further argued that such developments will contribute to the marginalization of the Christian faith.

Notice S IX 30, a verse in the Quran:

"The Jews call Uziar a son
Of God, and the Christians
Call Christ the Son of God.
That is a saying from their mounth;
(In this) they but imitate
What the Unbelievers of old
Used to say. God's curse
Be on them : how they are deluded
Away from the Truth!"

Muslims do not accept that Jesus is the Son of God, the Messiah promised by Moses. They accept Mohammed as their Messiah, promised by Moses. However, compare that to the clear instruction from the Bible:

"I have not written to you because you do not know the truth, but because you know it, and know that no lie is of the truth.
Who is a liar but he who denies that Jesus is the Christ? He who denies the Father and the Son is antichrist.
Everyone who denies the Son neither has the Father. The one confessing the Son also has the Father.
Therefore what you heard from the beginning, let it abide in you. If what you heard from the beginning remains in you,

you will abide in both the Son and in the Father."
(1 John 2:21-24, MKJV)

The reconciliation of differing faiths presents significant challenges. It is questionable whether political leaders can realistically expect these faiths to coexist peacefully within the same communities. The attempt by a monarch to serve as custodian of multiple faiths may inevitably lead to friction, social unrest, and potentially even acts of terrorism.

The blessings traditionally associated with Christian nations may be forfeited if these societies abandon Christian principles and enact legislation that excludes Christian values. There is an ongoing debate regarding whether English-speaking populations will be compelled to recognize other religions as equal or to accept a figure other than Jesus Christ as the Messiah. The theological implications of such changes, particularly regarding the role of Jesus and the historical significance of his crucifixion, raise important questions about national identity and religious tradition, especially if the British monarchy were to acknowledge another 'Messiah.'

"When Jehovah your God shall cut off the nations before you, where you go to possess them, and you take their place and dwell in their land,
take heed to yourself that you do not become snared by following them, after they are destroyed from before you, and that you do not ask about their gods, saying, How did these nations serve their gods, that I too may do likewise?

You shall not do so to Jehovah your God.
For every abomination to Jehovah, which
He hates, they have done to their gods;
even their sons and their daughters they
have burned in the fire to their gods.
All the things I command you, be careful
to do it. You shall not add to it, nor take
away from it."
(Deuteronomy 12:29-32, MKJV)

England appears to have lost sight of the reasons
for its historical blessings. There is an indication that even
the King may have neglected his responsibilities. The
continuity of the royal heritage is therefore uncertain. It is
questionable whether the monarch recognizes that he
cannot simultaneously serve as the custodian of both the
Christian faith of the Church of England and the Muslim
faith.

Historical accounts indicate that Ancient Israel
previously attempted to accommodate multiple faiths
within the nation, a strategy that ultimately proved
unsuccessful. On one occasion, a recognized Prophet of
God confronted the king regarding this issue as Israel
faced imminent invasion and the potential loss of its
national inheritance.

"And Elijah came to all the people and
said, How long are you limping over two
opinions? If Jehovah is God, follow Him.
But if Baal is God, then follow him. And
the people did not answer him a word."
(1 Kings 18:21, MKJV)

Throughout history, the kings of Israel frequently made significant concessions to accommodate other religions in pursuit of economic growth through international trade. These leaders permitted the establishment of alternative religious practices, often on elevated sites where structures were constructed for worship. Although these practices claimed to honor God, from a theological perspective, such actions were considered a form of religious infidelity.

> "I have seen your adulteries, and your neighings, the wickedness of your fornication, and your abominations on the hills in the fields. Woe to you, O Jerusalem! Will you not be made clean? How long will it still be?"
> (Jeremiah 13:27, MKJV)

God has not forgotten Ephraim and Manasseh, represented by Britain and America. These nations have received the blessings promised to Abraham in the present era. Historically, they dominated global affairs and were expected to disseminate Christianity worldwide. However, instances of misuse of power occurred. Currently, the monarch of England appears to have disregarded the divine source of their former greatness. Furthermore, there is an active promotion of practices contrary to traditional religious values.

> "Their doings will not allow them to turn to their God; for the spirit of fornication is in their midst, and they have not known Jehovah."
> (Hosea 5:4, MKJV)

Some commentators have expressed concerns regarding the potential for significant demographic and cultural changes in England, suggesting that increased immigration could lead to a perceived loss of national heritage. Additionally, there are claims that economic pressures may compel younger generations to seek employment abroad, which some interpret as a risk of economic dependency.

It has been argued by some that Christianity may face increasing marginalization in public institutions, including schools and workplaces, as religious diversity grows. There are also concerns about the proliferation of mosques and the visibility of Islamic practices in public spaces, which some perceive as indicative of broader societal changes.

Some perspectives suggest that increased political participation by Muslim individuals could alter the composition of the United Kingdom's government. Concerns have also been raised about the impact of migration, including the role of human traffickers and the provision of housing and employment for new arrivals. Critics argue that these developments may influence voting patterns and contribute to significant societal transformation.

> "So he shall act in the fortresses of the strongholds with a strange god, whom he shall acknowledge. He shall multiply in glory, and he shall cause them to rule over many, and shall divide the land for a price."
> (Daniel 11:39, MKJV)

It is predicted that the British Empire will experience a significant decline. After 2030, this decline is expected to accelerate, with similar patterns anticipated in Portugal and Spain, reminiscent of historical events from a millennium ago. Some forecasts suggest that groups from the South, particularly African Muslims supported by financial backers, may seek to expand their religious and political influence over the democratic systems of Britain and Northern Europe.

Some Christian leaders are expected to oppose perceived challenges to Christianity. However, it is anticipated that incidents of religiously motivated violence may increase, with some observers suggesting that these events could be minimized by certain leaders. Additionally, Christian leaders may face criticism and accusations of extremism or prejudice.

> "And I saw thrones, and they sat on them, and judgment was given to them. And I saw the souls of those who had been beheaded for the witness of Jesus and for the Word of God, and who had not worshiped the beast nor his image, nor had received his mark on their foreheads, nor in their hands. And they lived and reigned with Christ a thousand years."
> (Revelation 20:4, MKJV)

It is anticipated that the Islamic advance toward Rome may commence after 2030. In this context, Rome is expected to assume the role of the prophesied beast that will resist during the Last Days.

"And at the end-time, the king of the
south shall butt at him. And the king of
the north shall come against him like a
tempest, with chariots and with
horsemen and with many ships."
(Daniel 11:40, MKJV)

A coalition of Central European nations, along
with several Baltic states, is projected to form a strong
alliance, often referred to as a confederation of ten
leaders, to reclaim their territories from Islamic
occupation. This process is anticipated to involve
significant conflict. Additionally, the alliance is expected
to attempt to regain control of Israel and Jerusalem from
Islamic forces.

"And he shall enter into the countries
and shall overflow and pass over. He
shall also enter into the glorious land,
and many shall be stumbled. But these
shall escape out of his hand: Edom and
Moab, and the chief of the sons of
Ammon.
And he shall stretch out his hand on the
lands. And the land of Egypt shall not
escape.
But he shall have power over the
treasures of gold and silver, and over all
the precious things of Egypt. And the
Libyans and the Ethiopians shall be at
his steps."
(Daniel 11:41-43, MKJV)

Current events reflect concerns described in the prophecies of the Last Days. Many politicians appear to prioritize votes over their constituents' well-being, while some industry leaders focus on profit at the expense of worker safety and community welfare. The pursuit of cheap labor often takes precedence, with significant social and economic consequences, including cultural conflict and the potential destruction of property and businesses.

Amid these challenges, there appears to be little attention given to the sacrifice of Jesus Christ, which offers a path to salvation in God's Kingdom. Many seem indifferent to this opportunity for eternal life.

> "I am the door. If anyone enters in by Me, he shall be saved and shall go in and out and find pasture.
> The thief does not come except to steal and to kill and to destroy. I have come so that they might have life, and that they might have it more abundantly.
> I am the Good Shepherd. The Good Shepherd lays down His life for the sheep."
> (John 10:9-11, MKJV)

> "Everyone who denies the Son neither has the Father. The one confessing the Son also has the Father.
> Therefore what you heard from the beginning, let it abide in you. If what you heard from the beginning remains in you, you will abide in both the Son and in the Father.

And this is the promise that He has
promised us: everlasting life."
(1 John 2:23-25, MKJV)

Concerns have been raised about the future of religious freedom and national sovereignty in the United Kingdom and other regions. Some observers point to current events in countries such as Sudan, where religious minorities face persecution, as a warning. There are fears that political decisions and societal changes could pose increased challenges for certain faith communities and have significant social and cultural impacts.

Some express concern that demographic and cultural shifts in parts of Europe could lead to significant changes in religious and social structures. These concerns include the possibility of increased tensions and the potential for conflict if communities do not find ways to address differences peacefully.

There is apprehension that unresolved tensions could contribute to broader instability in the future.

Appendix C

Prophetic Timelines Intersect

We will now examine how biblical timelines relate to projections for the year 2030. According to some interpretations, significant geopolitical changes may occur, potentially affecting support for Israel and the security of Jerusalem. These perspectives suggest that such events could precede the anticipated return of the Messiah. Let us now review how the calendar aligns with these interpretations.

The timeline of Jonah

Let us revisit the Sign of Jonah, a prophet of almighty God. As noted earlier, **three days** were allotted for preaching, followed by **forty days** of grace for repentance.

"And Jonah arose and went to Nineveh, according to the Word of Jehovah. And Nineveh was a very great city of **three days'** journey.
And Jonah began to enter into the city a day's journey, and he cried and said, Yet **forty days** and Nineveh shall be overthrown!
And the people of Nineveh believed God. And they called a fast, and put on

sackcloth, from the greatest of them even to the least of them."
(Jonah 3:3-5, MKJV) [Emphasis mine]

The entire city of Nineveh repented of their corrupt practices, dishonest business dealings, and other sins that occur when people act as if there is no God. As a result, they were spared.

Timeline of Jesus' ministry (Day for a year)

Jesus preached in Jerusalem for three years, as indicated by the three Passovers He attended. His ministry spanned from 67 AD to 70 AD. Jerusalem was given **40 years** to repent, but did not. The people crucified Christ and sought to justify their actions. Forty years after the crucifixion, Jerusalem was destroyed, consistent with the day-for-a-year principle found in Ezekiel's prophecies.

"And when you have fulfilled them, lie again on your right side, and you shall bear the iniquity of the house of Judah forty days; **a day for a year**; a day for a year, I have set for you."
(Ezekiel4:6, MKJV) [Emphasis mine]

Timeline of Israel's Jubilees (Day for a Jubilee)

Three Jubilees before the first advent of the Messiah, the Temple was secured and daily sacrifices resumed. During this period, the Maccabees gained the right to worship according to the Law of Moses. The occupying forces recognized that granting the priesthood full religious freedom was necessary to avoid a major Jewish revolt, a lesson later understood by the Roman Empire during its occupation of Israel and Jerusalem.

For the last **three Jubilees,** Temple services testified against Israel's sin, and the sacrifices called for repentance. Israel was urged to repent and serve God until the Messiah arrived.

The pivotal moment marking the beginning of the further countdown is the ministry and crucifixion of Jesus Christ in 30 AD. Following this, **40 Jubilees** of hardship and banishment were declared for Israel. During this period, Jews faced ongoing opposition, including periods of oppression and events such as the Holocaust.

A Jubilee spans 50 years. Multiplying the 40-Jubilee period by 50 years results in 2,000 years. Counting from the crucifixion in 30 AD, this period concludes in **2030**.

Historical records indicate that after the banishment, the Northern Kingdom of Israel migrated through the Roman Empire and eventually settled in much of England. This group later became a significant sea power and controlled key strategic locations in recent times.

"that in blessing I will bless you, and in multiplying I will multiply your seed like the stars of the heavens, and as the sand which is upon the seashore. And your Seed shall **possess the gate of His enemies**."
(Genesis 22:17, ISV) [Emphasis mine]

Historically, England controlled territories such as the Suez Canal, Singapore, Gibraltar, Hong Kong, the Falkland Islands, Diego Garcia, Mauritius, St Helena, Ascension Island, Tristan da Cunha, and ports in South Africa, including Cape Town. In recent years, Britain has experienced a reduction in its overseas holdings. Some commentators attribute this shift to changes in national leadership and evolving social and religious dynamics. There are predictions that by 2030, Britain may face further challenges to its influence in Europe and beyond. These forecasts also suggest potential shifts in religious and cultural landscapes, with concerns about the future status of Christianity and other faith communities in the region.

Such will be the situation after 2030.

The Prophecies in Leviticus

While not widely recognized, the book of the Law contains prophecies and timelines that continue to have an impact. Leviticus 26 outlines several key promises.

God promised Israel significant blessings if they continued to worship Him, observe His Sabbaths and Holy Days, and follow the New Moon celebrations. Israel was expected to uphold the Covenant of the Ten Commandments and avoid pagan rituals and idolatry. The seventh-day Sabbath served as a sign of the Covenant, with Saturday worship symbolizing obedience. In contrast, Sunday and Friday were associated with pagan traditions that altered the original Covenant. If obedient, Israel would dwell securely in the Promised Land and experience abundant blessings.

> "You shall keep My sabbaths and revere
> My sanctuary. I am Jehovah.
> If you walk in My statutes and keep My
> commandments and do them,
> then I will give you rain in due season,
> and the land shall yield her increase, and
> the trees of the field shall yield their
> fruit."
> (Leviticus 26:2-4, MKJV)

Additional blessings would follow, including the prevention of disease and the absence of epidemics and pestilence. All efforts would be productive and contribute to an improved quality of life for everyone.

However, if they broke the Covenant by following other gods and adopting different rituals, God would withdraw blessings and permit hardships to affect their lives. They would be exiled from the Promised Land and, without continued observance of the Sabbath, risk losing their identity

The Northern Kingdom timeline

The Northern Kingdom of Israel, made up of ten tribes, broke the Covenant and was ultimately overthrown by its enemies. The Assyrians conquered the Northern Kingdom around 721 BC. In 701 BC, they besieged Jerusalem but withdrew. God protected the Southern Kingdom to encourage reflection and repentance based on the Northern Kingdom's fate. For a time, this approach was effective, and both the Southern Kingdom and Jerusalem were spared.

Therefore, the warnings from Leviticus were fulfilled in the Northern Kingdom.

"But if you will not listen to Me, and will
not do all these commandments,
and if you shall despise My statutes, or if
your soul hates My judgments, so that
you will not do all My commandments, so
that you break My covenant;
I will also do this to you: I will even
appoint terror over you, consumption,
and burning fever, consuming the eyes
and causing sorrow of heart. And you
shall sow your seed in vain, for your
enemies shall eat it.
And I will set My face against you, and
you shall be slain before your enemies.
They that hate you shall reign over you.
And you shall flee when none pursues
you."
(Leviticus 26:14-17, MKJV)

The year 700 BC marked a significant turning point. The ten tribes of the Northern Kingdom became known as the House of Israel, while the Southern Kingdom was called the House of Judah. The Assyrians occupied the Northern Kingdom, deported its people, and resettled foreigners in their place. These new inhabitants, known as the Sumerians, were generally disliked by those in the Southern Kingdom. The siege of Jerusalem in 701 BC ended any hope of reclaiming the Promised Land for the Northern Kingdom, making their banishment permanent by 700 BC.

Prophecies in Ezekiel.

The prophecies portrayed by Ezekiel provide more detail since the two Kingdoms became separated. We can glean more insight from Ezekiel 4.

"And you, son of man, take a tile to yourself, and lay it before you, and portray on it the city Jerusalem.
And lay siege against it, and build a fort against it, and cast a mound against it. Also set the camp against it, and set battering rams against it all around. And take an iron griddle to yourself, and set it for a wall of iron between you and the city. And set your face against it, and it shall be under attack. And you shall set a battle against it. This shall be a sign to the house of Israel.

Also lie on your left side, and lay the
iniquity of the house of Israel on it;
according to the number of days that you
shall lie on it, you shall bear their
iniquity.
For I have laid on you the years of their
iniquity, according to the number of the
days, **three hundred and ninety days**.
So you shall bear the iniquity of the
house of Israel."
(Ezekiel 4:1-5, MKJV) [Emphasis mine]

The Northern Kingdom, known as the House of
Israel, was exiled from the Promised Land for 390 years.
This period spans from 701 BC to 311 BC.

During the Wars of the Diadochi, the region of the
House of Israel became contested following the power
vacuum left by Alexander the Great. Although the area
could have been reclaimed, the ten tribes' neglect of the
Sabbaths led their descendants to lose awareness of their
heritage. As a result, the opportunity in 311 BC passed,
and the people of the Northern Kingdom faded further
into obscurity. Their banishment continued, and wherever
they settled, they faced ongoing challenges and
displacement. Over time, most eventually migrated to the
islands beyond Europe.

A further prophecy in Leviticus became effective:

"And if you will not yet listen to Me for all
this, then I will punish you seven times
more for your sins."
(Leviticus 26:18, MKJV)

If the banishment and hardship of the Northern Kingdom's tribes were multiplied by seven, what would be the resulting duration?

Multiplying 390 years by seven results in 2,730 years of exile from the Promised Land.

Adding 2,730 years to 701 BC, and accounting for the absence of a year zero, brings us to the year 2030. This result is noteworthy.

The Southern Kingdom timeline

Following the initial exile to Babylon, the prophet Daniel recognized from scripture that a return to the Promised Land would occur after 70 years. This opportunity was granted only to the Southern Kingdom. The tribes of Judah and Levi observed the Sabbaths while in exile and preserved their identity, which allowed them to return to Jerusalem. God provided them with another chance to build His Kingdom.

> "in the first year of his reign, I, Daniel, understood the number of the years by books, which came of the Word of Jehovah to Jeremiah the prophet, that he would accomplish seventy years in the desolations of Jerusalem."
> (Daniel 9:2, MKJV)

Daniel and his friends demonstrated loyalty to God and received His favor. King Darius later permitted the Jews to return to Jerusalem to rebuild the city and the Temple. Decades afterward, the Maccabees restored Temple worship for three Jubilees until the Messiah arrived as the eternal savior of humanity. This provided the Jews with another opportunity, but all of Jerusalem needed to repent from pagan practices and errors in worship.

Most Jews, influenced by their religious leaders and the occupying Roman authorities, rejected Jesus. The elite were responsible for His death. The people needed to recognize how far they had strayed from true worship, as they did not recognize the Son of God among them. Nevertheless, they were granted forty years to repent.

Notice the prophecies given to Ezekiel in this regard for the Southern Kingdom, the House of Judah.

> "And when you have fulfilled them, lie again on your right side, and you shall bear the iniquity of the house of Judah **forty days; a day for a year**; a day for a year, I have set for you.
> And you shall set your face toward the siege of Jerusalem, and your arm shall be uncovered, and you shall prophesy against it.
> And, behold, I will lay bands on you, and you shall not turn yourself from one side to another until you have ended the days of your siege."
> (Ezekiel 4:6-8, MKJV) [Emphasis mine]

These are separate prophecies. Therefore, Ezekiel was not instructed to repeatedly turn from one side to another. One prophecy concerns the House of Israel (the Northern Kingdom, 390 years), and the other concerns the House of Judah (the Southern Kingdom, Jerusalem, the Jews, 49 years).

The Temple needed to be prepared and available for the Messiah's First Advent. For three Jubilees, the Jews required authority in Jerusalem and the freedom to fully implement all Temple services. When Jesus arrived, events on earth mirrored those in Heaven, providing lessons about spiritual realities. The sequence was therefore restarted for Judah and Jerusalem. Jesus represented their best opportunity. If Judah had repented and followed Jesus, God could have intervened, forcing the Romans to leave the Promised Land. This is what the Apostles understood. According to the prophecies of Jonah and Ezekiel, Jerusalem was given 40 years to repent. However, this did not occur, and the offender was banished. Jerusalem was besieged, overthrown, and the Temple destroyed, all of which took place 40 years after Jesus' ministry, in 70 AD.

For how many years would Jews and Covenant Christians who observed the Sabbaths be prevented from occupying Jerusalem and inheriting the Promised Land? The first possible opportunity to return would come seven times later. Refer to the next warning in Leviticus 26.

"then I will walk contrary to you and will punish you seven times more for your sins."
(Leviticus 26:24, MKJV)

These are distinct prophecies. Ezekiel was not instructed to repeatedly alternate sides. One prophecy addresses the House of Israel (the Northern Kingdom, 390 years), while the other concerns the House of Judah (the Southern Kingdom, Jerusalem, the Jews, 49 years).

The Temple needed to be ready for the Messiah's First Advent. For three Jubilees, the Jews required authority in Jerusalem and the freedom to conduct all

Temple services. When Jesus arrived, earthly events reflected those in Heaven, offering spiritual lessons. As a result, the sequence was restarted for Judah and Jerusalem. Jesus was their greatest opportunity. Had Judah repented and followed Jesus, God could have intervened and removed the Romans from the Promised Land. The Apostles understood this. According to the prophecies of Jonah and Ezekiel, Jerusalem was given 40 years to repent. Since this did not happen, the offender was banished. Jerusalem was besieged, overthrown, and the Temple destroyed 40 years after Jesus' ministry, in 70 AD.

For how many years would Jews and Covenant Christians who observed the Sabbaths be prevented from occupying Jerusalem and inheriting the Promised Land? The first opportunity to return would come seven times later. See the next warning in Leviticus 26.

.

"And if you will not for all of this listen to Me, but will walk contrary to Me,
then I will walk contrary to you also in fury. And I, even I, will chastise you
seven times for your sins."
(Leviticus 26:27-28, MKJV)

If we multiply the time period by 7 again, we arrive at 40 x 7 x 7, which equals 1,960 years. Adding 1,960 to 70 AD brings us to the year 2030.

What are the implications for the House of Judah? Jewish communities are present worldwide, and there has been a noted rise in anti-Semitism. Changes in government leadership in countries allied with Israel may affect support for Jewish communities. The safety and future of the House of Judah remain important concerns.

Many believe that, ultimately, the Messiah will return to protect the House of Judah.

European Timeline

Rome governed Europe and, in response to the spread of Christianity, established a form of Christianity that incorporated elements of paganism to unify diverse faiths within the Empire. While this may have served political interests, such practices were not consistent with the original teachings of Christianity and are contrary to Christian scripture.

> "Beloved, when I gave all diligence to write unto you of the common salvation, it was needful for me to write unto you, and exhort you that ye should earnestly contend for the faith which was once delivered unto the saints.
> For there are certain men crept in unawares, who were before of old ordained to this condemnation, ungodly men, turning the grace of our God into **lasciviousness**, and denying the only Lord God, and our Lord Jesus Christ."
> (Jude 1:3-4, KJV) [Emphasis mine]

It was suggested that grace permits lawlessness and that the Commandments, the Biblical calendar, and Biblical festivals were abolished. As a result, generations of Christians were denied access to these timelines. This outcome was prophesied.

"And he shall speak great words against the most High, and shall wear out the saints of the most High, and think to change times and laws: and they shall be given into his hand until a time and times and the dividing of time."
(Daniel 7:25, MKJV)

The Christianity that Rome developed changed from Sabbath to Sunday, from Passover to Easter, and from the Feast of Tabernacles to Xmas. All these festivals proposed by the European church were all done on different dates, all on a different calendar. These changes happened through several Councils, the first being the Council of Nicaea in 325 AD. While these changes were being promulgated from Rome, a new bishop, Cyril, would lead to renewal and opportunities for Christians and Jews in Jerusalem. This was the time a notable miracle happened in 351 AD, after the Passover season, when a luminous cross appeared over Jerusalem. It was a lost opportunity to return to the original Faith. Rome went further with more Councils, further changing Christian doctrine.

In 536 AD, major volcanic eruptions caused a severe and prolonged winter across the Northern Hemisphere. This event led to a mini ice age, resulting in widespread crop failures and famine. Despite these challenges, the Roman Emperor and the Pope in Rome formed a strategic alliance to maintain control over the Empire, finalizing their unification in 538 AD. Rather than reconsidering their approach, Rome convened additional Councils, moving further from its original faith and initiating the period described as the "time, times, and half a time" of Papal rule, as referenced by the prophet Daniel.

A "time" in prophecy is understood as a year, with each year consisting of 360 days according to Biblical tradition, as seen in Genesis 8. Multiplying 360 by three and a half yields 1,260, which is interpreted as 1,260 years of Papal rule, as referenced in the book of Daniel. This era is commonly known as the Dark Middle Ages in Europe. The Papal absolute rule ended in 1798, when French General Louis-Alexandre Berthier captured Pope Pius VI, thereby ending papal authority over civil affairs. After this period, European monarchs regained supremacy.

Several prophecies are expected to unfold after 2030. Europe is anticipated to play a more prominent role, with Germany and Italy increasing their military capabilities. Tensions between Islamic and Christian communities in the Western world may escalate, potentially leading to conflict involving Jerusalem.

The purpose of this book is to demonstrate that significant global changes are expected around the year 2030, marking the approach of what some consider the Last Days.

Appendix D

WW3?

Global conflicts are expected to escalate, potentially involving more nations. This raises questions about the possibility of a final world war and the signs that may indicate its approach. We will examine these signs in detail, noting that some are already evident while others may develop into significant global issues.

When asked about these events, Jesus provided several indications. Some were fulfilled locally during the time of the apostles, while similar developments are anticipated to occur globally today. Additionally, the fulfillment of the Prophet Daniel's vision remains significant. We will review each of these signs.

Daniel's Vision Resurrected

According to Daniel's prophecy, four kingdoms would arise between Daniel's era and the Messiah's First Advent, each posing a threat to Jerusalem. These kingdoms are expected to reemerge collectively in the Last Days.

1) Iraq is expected to revive its traditional form of Islam and seek greater global influence. Similar to ancient Babylon, it may integrate various Islamic ideas to counter the more radical form of Islam emerging from Iran. International actors may support efforts to oppose radical jihadist movements. Iraq may also seek to reduce Western

influence, particularly by targeting American military presence, and could eventually assert claims over Jerusalem.

2) Iran is considered a significant concern due to its support for terrorism and arms proliferation. Like the historical Medo-Persian Empire, it poses a growing threat to Jerusalem and regional stability. Its nuclear capabilities are advancing, increasing the perceived threat. Iran has successfully promoted its radical form of Islam, but this may be challenged by a more moderate movement emerging from Iraq. Iran has also expressed intentions regarding Jerusalem.

3) Greece is anticipated to form alliances with other Balkan states, particularly those with historical ties to Macedonia. These Central European nations may seek to revive the influence of the Greco-Macedonian Empire, forming a third power bloc as described in Daniel's vision. The conflict in Ukraine may accelerate this process, and the region's Orthodox Christian tradition may also assert claims over Jerusalem.

4) Rome is projected to unify Western Europe and may marginalize Protestant Christianity within the region. Having incorporated various traditions, it may seek to promote Roman Catholicism and challenge Protestant influence, particularly in English-speaking nations. Rome may then position itself as the protector of Jerusalem.

According to Revelation, these four kingdoms and their associated religions will regain prominence. The spiritual forces that once influenced these kingdoms were restrained to prevent further conflict until the Last Days, when they will be released. In response to threats from Gog and Magog, these kingdoms may seek to revive former strategies and beliefs to regain influence.

"When the sixth angel blew his trumpet, I heard a voice from the four horns of the gold altar in front of God.
It told the sixth angel who had the trumpet, "Release the four angels who are held at the great Euphrates River."
So the four angels who were ready for that hour, day, month, and year were released to kill one-third of humanity.
The number of cavalry troops was 200,000,000. I heard how many there were."
(Revelation 9:13-16, ISV)

Certain forms of religious enforcement are already established, while others are still emerging and may face opposition. For example, a more moderate form of Islam may accept some human rights concepts. Iraq is also expected to address the presence of American bases on its territory. Ultimately, each of the four religious influences will seek authority within its respective regions and may claim a stake in Jerusalem. However, according to Christian belief, Jesus will return and challenge all these claims.

Nebuchadnezzar's vision depicted a succession of world powers that would lose influence over time. In contrast, the prophet Daniel foresaw a spiritual dynamic in which these influences would reemerge and coexist in the Last Days, with all four present at the Second Advent of Christ. These groups will oppose one another, leading to conflict across various regions. When the Messiah arrives and challenges their beliefs, they will unite against Christ and gather the world's armies in Jerusalem. The prophet's vision indicates that all elements of the statue will be destroyed together in the end.

"You watched until a stone was cut out without hands, which struck the image upon its feet which were of iron and clay, and broke them to pieces.

Then the iron, the clay, the bronze, the silver, and the gold were broken to pieces **together.** And they became like the chaff of the summer threshing floors. And the wind carried them away, so that no place was found for them. And the stone that struck the image became a great mountain and filled the whole earth."

(Daniel 2:34-35, MKJV) [Emphasis mine]

The four major faiths will assemble their armies against Jerusalem. When global forces unite under these four faiths and move toward Jerusalem, it will signal the onset of the final World War.

"And when you see Jerusalem compassed with armies, then know that its destruction has come."

(Luke 21:20, MKJV)

"And in that day I will make Jerusalem a burdensome stone for all peoples. All who lift it shall be slashed, and all the nations of the earth will be gathered against it."

(Zechariah 12:3, MKJV)

The gathering of international armies is expected to spark civil unrest and conflict across many countries. Political leaders have supported global migration and integration among diverse groups, which may heighten tensions if conflict arises over Jerusalem.

"And it shall be in that day I will seek to destroy all the nations that come against Jerusalem.

And I will pour on the house of David, and on the people of Jerusalem, the spirit of grace and of prayers. And they shall look on Me whom they have pierced, and they shall mourn for Him, as one mourns for his only son, and shall be bitter over Him, as the bitterness over the first-born."

(Zechariah 12:9-10, MKJV)

Christ will return and confront a world that has long rejected Him. According to prophecy, subsequent events of the Second Coming will unfold. Some individuals will repent and worship the God and Father of Jesus Christ, while most military forces will continue to rely on their technology and will ultimately be defeated.

A key factor is the removal of Western military bases from Iraq, which would allow for the rebuilding of Babylon. Additionally, it is important for moderate and diverse Islamic groups to unite and respond to opposing faiths globally.

We should also consider the sequence of events Jesus described during His prophecy on the Mount of Olives. After the disciples remarked on the Temple's grandeur, Jesus unexpectedly predicted its destruction, prompting them to ask for further explanation.

> "And as He sat on the Mount of Olives, the disciples came to Him privately, saying, Tell us, when shall these things be? And what shall be the sign of Your coming, and of the end of the world?"
>
> (Matthew 24:3, MKJV)

Two questions were presented to Jesus Christ, and He provided two distinct answers. First, He addressed the situation in Jerusalem at that time. Second, He spoke about the events of the Last Days before His Second Advent.

> "And Jesus answered and said to them, Take heed that no man deceive you.
>
> For many will come in My name, saying, I am Christ, and will deceive many."
>
> (Matthew 24:4-5, MKJV)

Numerous Christian movements and churches may emerge under the name of Christ, though some may be deceptive and promote a different Gospel.

> "And you will hear of wars and rumors of wars. See that you are not troubled, for all these things must occur; but the end is not yet.

For nation will rise against nation, and kingdom against kingdom. And there will be famines and pestilences and earthquakes in different places.

All these are the beginning of sorrows."

(Matthew 24"6-8, MKJV)

A similar situation occurred in the first century, when the Roman Empire faced significant opposition following its involvement in the crucifixion of Jesus. In response, some leaders resorted to severe measures, including atrocities against early Christians, to maintain control. It is possible that comparable circumstances could arise in the Last Days.

As conflicts persist and more nations become involved, increasing sanctions may restrict economic growth. Supply chain disruptions are likely, which could drive up food prices and lead to famines. Additionally, the ongoing threat of climate change remains a significant concern.

"And this gospel of the kingdom shall be proclaimed in all the world as a witness to all nations. And then the end shall come."

(Matthew 24:14, MKJV)

The Internet now enables the true Gospel to be shared globally. However, if government censorship prevents its proclamation, this would signal the arrival of the Last Days. At that point, if oppression by elites renders life unbearable, there would be no reason for God to allow the current world to continue.

"Therefore when you see the abomination of desolation, spoken of by Daniel the prophet, stand in the holy place (whoever reads, let him understand)."
(Matthew 24:15, MKJV)

This will occur both spiritually and physically. Sacrifices may resume on or near the Temple Mount in Jerusalem. If the Jewish people are compelled to offer unclean sacrifices, as occurred in 70 AD, it will mark the arrival of the Last Days. This event will repeat when the so-called King of the North desecrates the Altar in Jerusalem.

"And forces will stand from him, and they will profane the sanctuary, the fortress, and shall remove the daily sacrifice, and they shall place the desolating abomination."
(Daniel 11:31, MKJV)

When this occurs, World War III will follow, leaving only a few years until the supernatural return of Jesus Christ, the Messiah.
"And from the time that the daily sacrifice shall be taken away, and the desolating abomination set up, a thousand two hundred and ninety days shall occur."
(Daniel 12:11, MKJV)

This occurred previously, prompting the disciples to flee to Petra. It may happen again in the near future, as Jesus described. He warned that many false church leaders will claim to be the returned Messiah, but His return will be unmistakably supernatural.

> "Therefore if they shall say to you,
> Behold, He is in the desert! Do not go
> out. Behold, He is in the secret rooms!
> Do not believe it.
> For as the lightning comes out of the east
> and shines even to the west, so also will
> be the coming of the Son of Man."
> (Matthew 24:26-27, MKJV)

Jesus will descend from heaven and appear above the clouds. As the earth turns and television broadcasts the event, people worldwide will witness the miracle firsthand. There will be no doubt. Jesus gave a profound indication:

> "Now learn a parable of the fig tree. When
> its branch is still tender and puts out
> leaves, you know that summer is near.
> So you, likewise, when you see all these
> things, shall know that it is near, at the
> doors.
> Truly I say to you, This generation shall
> not pass until all these things are
> fulfilled."
> (Matthew 24:32-34, MKJV)

Jesus was referring directly to Jerusalem and, by extension, to Israel. Matthew 21 provides context: the people of Jerusalem honored Jesus for His healings, while the priesthood, driven by jealousy, sought to undermine Him. Jesus illustrated this through the parable of the fig tree, which withered when found fruitless. Later, in Matthew 24, He referenced the fig tree again, now sprouting leaves, symbolizing renewed growth and expanding influence.

The modern state of Israel is still young and seeks to expand its borders, which may lead to conflict with neighboring Muslim populations. Certain verses in the Quran anticipate resistance if Muslims are displaced from Jerusalem. Such developments are considered signs of the Last Days.

This also reflects a global trend, as nations and former powers seek to expand or reclaim territory, leading to conflicts and wars. The generation living during a time when elites pursue power through harmful means will face the final war of the Last Days. Many will perish, but survivors will witness the supernatural return of the Messiah. At that time, all other religions, including those that falsely claim Christianity, will be disproven, leaving no doubt about the true faith.

The remainder of Matthew 24 is understood primarily by the saints in the Churches of God. Nevertheless, signs of the Last Days are evident to all. Many will continue their lives unaware of the impending conflict, as prophesied. Widespread disinterest in the Bible was also foretold, with atheism spreading through the theory of macroevolution. Many do not realize that civilizations built on greed and environmental degradation will ultimately face hunger and famine. This situation cannot continue indefinitely.

"But as the days of Noah were, so shall be the coming of the Son of Man.
For as in the days before the flood, they were eating and drinking, marrying and

giving in marriage, until the day Noah entered into the ark."
(Matthew 24:37-38)

Are we at a WW3 situation?

While this event remains several years away, we continue to anticipate the return of the Messiah, the Son of God, whose significance is often overlooked.

The situation in the Middle East has worsened. Arab countries near the Bab el-Mandeb Strait and the Strait of Hormuz may threaten shipping bound for the Suez Canal. Nearly half of Europe's trade passes through this section of the Red Sea, and a third of global oil supply transits the Persian Gulf. Many ships are now rerouted around the Cape of Good Hope, causing significant delays and increased shipping costs to Europe. With ongoing fuel inflation and a cost-of-living crisis, these disruptions could push more Europeans into poverty. The European Union faces the challenge of maintaining internal stability amid these economic pressures and a significant influx of migrants from affected regions.

The EU and NATO have established a joint naval presence in the region to protect commercial shipping. If the situation remains unresolved, Europe may become increasingly involved in the Middle East conflict, potentially escalating tensions worldwide.

Rising incidents of anti-Semitism and terrorist attacks in some European countries have heightened concerns about public safety and social cohesion. Political leaders now face the challenge of addressing these security risks while upholding human rights. Escalating food prices and internal tensions could further strain relations among different communities. The ongoing conflict may also impact migrants and their families in both Europe and their countries of origin.

Some interpret current events as aligning with the prophecies of Daniel 11, viewing the EU and NATO as the 'King of the North' and Arab nations as the 'King of the South.' Ongoing conflicts over trade, migration, and religious differences may be seen as fulfilling these prophecies. The escalation of hostilities in key maritime regions could be viewed as part of this sequence. Consider the following scriptures:

> "And now I will declare to you the truth. Behold, there shall stand up yet three kings in Persia. And the fourth shall be far richer than all of them. And by his strength, through his riches, he shall stir up all against the kingdom of Greece."

> (Daniel 11:2, MKJV)

At that time, Greece was considered the King of the North. Currently, the European Union is viewed as fulfilling this role according to the prophecy.

> "For the king of the north shall return, and shall send out a multitude greater than the former, and at the end of times, years, shall come with a great army and with much equipment."

> (Daniel 11:13, MKJV)

Countries influenced by the Muslim Brotherhood are expected to form a unified bloc, known as the King of the South. This development should be considered from Israel's perspective, especially in Jerusalem.

> "And he shall stir up his power and his heart against the king of the south with a great army. And the king of the south shall be stirred up to battle with a very great and mighty army, but he shall not stand. For they shall devise plots against him."

(Daniel 11:25, MKJV)

Recent migration patterns in Europe have raised concerns about the potential for radicalization and internal security risks. Some analysts suggest that European nations supporting Israel may face increased threats of domestic terrorism. The presence of individuals with opposing allegiances within national borders is viewed by some as a significant security challenge.

> "And at the end-time, the king of the south shall butt at him. And the king of the north shall come against him like a tempest, with chariots and with horsemen and with many ships."

(Daniel 11:40, MKJV)

Religious conflicts

The current conflicts are not solely political; religious factors also play a significant role. It is important to examine the religious differences between the peoples associated with the kings of the north and south. Additionally, understanding the distinctions between Islam and general Christianity, with Judaism as a central influence, provides further insight.

The Bible does not address Islam directly, as Islam emerged more than 600 years after Christianity. Therefore, there are no explicit references to Islam. However, some scriptural passages warn against apostasy from core Christian beliefs.

In contrast, Islamic scriptures address both Judaism and Christianity extensively. Mohammed was familiar with these major faiths and offered significant critiques. In the Quran, the term "Believers" refers specifically to followers of Mohammed and adherents of Islam. The following are examples from the Quran:

"Strongest among men in enmity
To the Believers wilt though
Find the Jews and Pagans;
And nearest among them in love
To the Believers wilt thou
Find those who say,
"We are Christians" :
Because among these are
Men devoted to learning
And men who have renounced

The world, and they
Are not arrogant."
(Sura v, 85)

Historical tensions between religious groups in the Middle East have contributed to ongoing conflict and mistrust. While some individuals from different faiths collaborate, longstanding differences continue to influence attitudes and can escalate tensions.

Some political leaders suggest that different faiths can coexist peacefully. However, religious texts reflect significant theological differences. For example, Islam teaches that Jesus is not the Son of God, which contrasts with core Christian beliefs. These differences can present challenges to interfaith understanding.

"The Jews call Uzair a son
Of God, and the Christians
Call Christ the Son of God.
That is a saying from their mouth;
(In this) They but imitate
What the Unbelievers of old
Used to say. God's curse
Be on them : how they are deluded
Away from the truth!"
(Sura ix, 30)

Some Jews regarded Ezra, also known as Uzair, as a son of God, possibly because of his prophecies and leadership in rebuilding the Temple. However, this view is not supported by the Bible. The Bible clearly identifies Jesus Christ as **the** Son of God, and belief in Him as the Son of God sent from Heaven is central to the Christian faith.

"and every spirit that does not confess that Jesus Christ has come in the flesh is not of God. And this is the antichrist you heard is coming, and even now is already in the world."
(1 John 4:3, MKJV)

The differences among Jews, Christians, and Muslims are significant and deeply rooted in their respective scriptures and teachings. These fundamental disagreements can intensify as adherents study their faiths more closely. In some cases, tensions have arisen in Western communities, and there are concerns about the potential for radicalization. Policymakers must remain vigilant to address these challenges and promote social cohesion.

Conflict in Israel between Jewish and Muslim communities may further destabilize the region. Neighboring countries could become involved, potentially escalating tensions throughout the Middle East. Such developments may threaten shipping routes, disrupt oil supplies, and impact global supply chains. Western nations might be compelled to intervene to protect international trade, increasing the risk of broader international involvement.

Religious differences have the potential to contribute to global conflicts and may serve as catalysts for broader confrontations.

Many believe that resolving these deep-seated differences requires guidance from a divinely authorized figure. For Christians, Jesus Christ is seen as uniquely qualified to fulfill this role, having demonstrated unwavering loyalty to God and love for humanity.

Some interpret current events in the Middle East as fulfilling prophecies in Daniel 12, anticipating significant developments leading up to the Second Advent of Christ.

Political conflicts

The war in Ukraine highlights the ongoing conflict between differing forms of governance. Western nations, led by the European Union and supported by NATO, are expanding their influence eastward. The EU and UN advocate for human rights, including those of the LGBTQ+ community, which contrasts with the values held by some Eastern and Southern societies. These differences contribute to ongoing tensions.

In contrast, some states with centralized governments, including members of the BRICS alliance, seek to protect their interests and expand their global influence. These countries represent a range of religious and secular perspectives. The conflict in Ukraine reflects broader ideological divisions, and there is concern that it could escalate as more nations become involved.

While it may be possible to de-escalate current conflicts, significant challenges remain. Ongoing geopolitical shifts, economic alliances, climate change, and migration are likely to shape future global dynamics. These factors may increase tensions between nations and cultures, highlighting the need for effective leadership and cooperation.

The potential for future large-scale conflict remains uncertain. Ongoing developments will require close observation. An eventual worldwide conflict is a possibility. The warning is even more applicable today than ever before:

"The heaven and the earth shall
pass away, but My Words shall not
pass away.
And take heed to yourselves, lest
your hearts are weighed down with
headaches and drinking and
anxieties of this life; and that day
should suddenly come on you;
for it shall come as a snare on all
those sitting on the face of the
whole earth.
Watch therefore, praying in every
season that you may be counted
worthy to escape all these things
which shall occur, and to stand
before the Son of Man."
(Luke 21:33-36, MKJV)

www.ingramcontent.com/pod-product-compliance
Lightning Source LLC
Chambersburg PA
CBHW021210160726

47994CB00001B/415